STILL GOING STRONG

a history of
SCOTCH WHISKY
ADVERTISING

JOHN HUGHES

STILL GOING STRONG

a history of SCOTCH WHISKY ADVERTISING

TEMPUS

First published 2005

Tempus Publishing Ltd
The Mill, Brimscombe Port
Stroud, Gloucestershire GL5 2QG
www.tempus-publishing.com

British Library Cataloguing in Publication Data.
A catalogue record for this book is available from the British Library.

ISBN 0 7524 2174 9

Typesetting, design and origination by Tempus Publishing.

Contents

Dedication

This book is dedicated to my wife Juliet and to Alice, Mike and Tom.

Acknowledgements

When I was researching material to illustrate my first book, *Scotland's Malt Whisky Distilleries*, I discovered the rich resource of advertising and other historical material in Diageo's Archive at Menstrie in Stirlingshire. The co-operation and assistance given to me in the preparation of material contained in *Still Going Strong* by Patrick Millet of Diageo plc in London, and Archivist Christine Jones and her colleagues in the company's Archive, has been outstanding and made my task a pleasure.

To them I raise a glass of the finest blended Scotch whisky, likely to be one born in 1820, and say 'Many, many thanks. Slainte!'

Chapter 1
Scotch Whisky's Difficult History

THE ILLUSTRATED LONDON NEWS, June 26, 1897.— 899

Pattisons' WHISKY
Victorious all along the line

A BIG BOOM

THE BOOMING OF THE CANNON

is nothing to the "booming" of Pattisons' Whisky. Steady unfaltering attention to the object aimed at hits the mark and wins the battle. Pattisons have aimed at hitting the public taste for a pure, sound, fully matured, delicately flavoured whisky, and they have succeeded. Pattisons' Whisky is the Scotch spirit in its perfection—wholesome, stimulating, and cream-like. Pattisons' Whisky has fought its way to the front and will remain there.

Sole Proprietors:

PATTISONS, Ltd., Highland Distillers, **BALLINDALLOCH, LEITH, AND LONDON.**
Head Offices: CONSTITUTION STREET, LEITH.

1897. From boom to bust. The size and extent of the scandal and financial failure that followed the collapse of Pattison's in December 1898, marked the end of the most discreditable chapter in the history of the whisky trade.

The Act of Parliament known as the Blending Act of 1865 gave an enormous stimulus to the Scotch whisky industry by allowing malt and grain whiskies to be blended together. Many new blended whiskies were created, individually uniform in character, milder and smoother than many of the strongly flavoured malts and therefore with a broader appeal. At first, most of the blended whiskies were sold in small casks for use as 'own labels' by grocers, wine merchants and brewers. It was during the 1870s and 1880s that the development plans were being put in place of the brands of blended whiskies that were destined to dominate the world markets during the twentieth century. In most cases, blends such as *Johnnie Walker, Haig, VAT 69, White Horse* and *Buchanan Blend*, the forerunner of *Black & White*, having become well established in Scotland, were then sold into England through sales offices established in London and large provincial towns. There are many stories of the painstaking efforts placed behind selling the brands to the licensed trade and influential private customers. It was not only in Britain that considerable effort was being made to stimulate sales of blended whiskies. During the 1880s and 1890s the brand owners made some extraordinary and lengthy sales journeys round the world, developing enthusiasm for their whiskies and establishing networks of sales agencies and distributors.

The last decade of the nineteenth century was probably the most exciting and dramatic chapter to date in the history of the whisky industry. To satisfy the demand from the blenders for more and more malt whisky, many old and established distilleries were enlarged or totally rebuilt. Thirty-three new distilleries were built in Scotland during the l890s, of which twenty-one were on Speyside, an area in north-east Scotland midway between Inverness and Aberdeen, through which flows the river Spey and its many tributaries, including the Livet and Fiddich. The blenders were supplying smooth and mellow whiskies to their customers and favoured the delicate flavour and finesse of the Speyside malts – a fashion that remains to this day.

The rapid growth in exports and the rush to build new

distilleries at the end of the nineteenth century led almost inevitably to speculation and over-production. The Pattison brothers, Robert and Walter, began their business life as partners in a grocery business in Leith. In 1887 they embarked on whisky blending and converted to become a public company in 1896, based, as it later transpired, on a fraudulent balance sheet. They sold mainly within the home market and their whisky was widely advertised. The company had borrowed heavily from several banks but their activities, mainly based on fraud, spurious information, falsified accounts and payment of dividends from capital, led them to suspend payment to their creditors on 6 December 1898. Pattison's subsequent bankruptcy affected the whole industry. Several companies went bankrupt as a result of the affair and the country was awash with surplus stocks of whisky. The Pattison brothers were jailed for fraud and embezzlement and no new distillery was to be built for the next fifty years.

The first years of the twentieth century saw the onset of a period of economic depression following the end of the Boer War, and the death of Queen Victoria, a significant supporter of the industry during her long reign. Whisky sales declined in the home market and although the hangover of post-Pattison stocks was slowly being corrected, almost a quarter of Scotland's distilleries had stopped making whisky by 1910. There were, however, encouraging signs for the whisky industry with steadily increasing export sales to Australia, South Africa, India, the United States and Canada.

During that first decade there was considerable debate as to the legal definition of whisky. For four years, between July 1905 and July 1909, a number of events occurred that led to a legal challenge to establish 'What is Whisky?'. In July 1905 the London Borough of Islington Council served notices on a number of members of the Off-Licences Association for selling blended whisky containing patent still (grain) spirit adjudged by the magistrate hearing the subsequent case that 'such spirit was not whisky' – in short, that blending malt whisky with grain spirit constituted adulteration. This action created consternation

1906. Cambus distillery in Clackmannanshire first produced malt whisky in 1806 and was converted to being a grain distillery in 1836. The Moubray family ran the distillery and the company became a founder member of The Distillers Company Limited in 1877. The distillery ceased production in 1992.

(right) 1907. At a time when DCL had a huge amount to lose if the 'What is Whisky' argument went against the producers of grain whisky, DCL's own *Cambus* was strongly advertised during 1906 and 1907. There was to be no doubt that *Cambus* was not from a pot still – it was unmixed with any pot still whisky whatever and was unashamedly a Pure Patent Still Scotch Grain Whisky. It had purity and had been matured in wood for at least seven years, and at 3*s* 6*d* (17.5p) a bottle it was 'The Clear Head Bottle' with 'Not a headache in a gallon'.

(far right) 1915. Following the 1915 Immature Spirits Act that discontinued the sale of whisky until it had been matured for a minimum of two years, J & G Stewart were quick to advertise that they held sufficient stocks of mature whisky to cope with the restrictions imposed by the Act. Their range of three whiskies varied in age between seven and fifteen years old. The company was acquired by DCL in 1917.

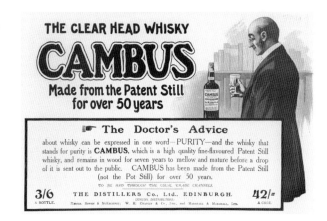

within the whisky industry and the licensed trade and, after lengthy legal argument and much protestation, a Royal Commission was appointed in February 1908.

To the fore in the argument, and hiring an advertising agency to prepare propaganda in favour of the product of the patent still, was a company that was in due course to become the largest drinks company in the world. The Distillers Co. Ltd – familiarly known as DCL – had been established in 1877 by six of the largest grain whisky distillers with the main purpose of protecting themselves against other grain distillers in England, Ireland and Germany. Now they had to defend their interests in a case that could lead to discrimination in favour of malt whisky. With a budget of £4,000, *Cambus* pure grain whisky, sold under DCL's label, was the brand selected for use in an advertising campaign defending the fine quality and other virtues of pure patent still Scotch grain whisky.

It was a position worth defending. In 1909 the Royal Commission concluded that:

> the term 'whiskey' having been recognised in the past as applicable to a potable spirit manufactured from (1) malt, (2) malt and unmalted barley or other cereals, the application of the term 'whiskey' should not be denied to the product manufactured from such materials.

The Commission found no evidence that the form of the still had any relation to the wholesomeness of spirit, and it was

(far left) 1919. Haig & Haig strongly criticised the Government's policy of limiting sales by retailers to those customers who were in the country in 1916. This, they argued, allowed conscientious objectors to drink their 1916 ration of whisky, but the men who saved the country and lived to return to Britain could not. *Haig & Haig Five Stars Scots Whisky* was the forerunner to *Dimple Scots*, which made its first appearance under that brand name in 1923.

(left) 1922. Haig & Haig took a full page in *Punch* to continue their campaign against the unfairness of the 1920 imposition of duty at 8s 5½d (42.3p) a bottle, over four times the level before the war. This level of duty combined with the impact of a decade of economic recession that affected Britain during the 1920s, and a change in the social attitudes to drinking, had by 1930 reduced consumption of spirits by a quarter.

unable to recommend that the use of the word 'whiskey' should be restricted to spirit manufactured by the pot still process. At last there was a satisfactory conclusion to a controversy that had increasingly concerned malt whisky and grain whisky distillers alike for a number of years.

Further difficulties were heaped on the whisky industry in Lloyd George's People's Budget of 1909, when the duty on whisky was increased by over one-third from 11*s* (55p) to 14*s* 6*d* (72.5p) per proof gallon. There were loud protestations from the trade. Peter Mackie, of the *White Horse* firm Mackie & Co., declared: 'The whole framing of the Budget is that of a faddist and a crank and not a statesman. But what can one expect of a Welsh country solicitor being played, without any commercial training, as Chancellor of the Exchequer in a large country like this?'. The Budget had a catastrophic effect on sales. More than twenty distilleries closed, whisky brokers and merchants failed and in order that they might have a chance of survival, a number of blending companies merged.

The First World War began on 4 August 1914 and it was generally believed that it would be over by Christmas. It was not, and as the war escalated Lloyd George declared: 'Drink is doing more damage in the war than all the German submarines put together'. State purchase of the liquor trade was considered but ruled out on the

basis of the enormous cost estimated at £225 million. In May 1915 he set up the Central Control Board to limit the number of retail outlets in areas where munitions were manufactured and to make recommendations to control liquor consumption. The opening hours of licensed premises were cut by half in Scotland and by two-thirds in England and Wales. The state took over licensed premises and the control of brewing in three areas where there were large munitions factories: Carlisle and Enfield in England and Invergordon in north-east Scotland. Among other regulations, the Board directed that whisky had to be sold at strengths no higher than 35° under proof (37.2 per cent alcohol by volume) . In his Budget of the same year, Lloyd George proposed doubling the rate of duty on spirits. Howls of protest from the drink trade eventually secured the replacement of the threatened duty increase

1923. The activities of the Temperance movement and Prohibition in the United States were of obvious concern to the whisky industry and they spawned several carefully orchestrated advertisements using professional medical endorsements of the beneficial and healthy effects of moderate use of whisky. A number of brands counselled the safe use of whisky. In a number of advertisements during 1923 and 1924, *King William IV Six Stars Scots Whisky* promoted cautious consumption and brand quality in the simple line 'A Little and Good', the same words as used by *Haig & Haig Five Stars Scots Whisky* in their 1922 advertisement.

The Professor of Vital Statistics in the School of Hygiene and Public Health at Baltimore's John Hopkins University was quoted as stating that to drink in moderation is preferable to abstention, and that it is wise to pay a little extra for a better quality whisky. Furthermore, foreign markets yield a better profit and the duty at 8s 5½d (42.3p) per bottle is a terrible handicap on a great Home industry and a great injustice to Scotland. 'A Little and Good' is the message, and this is followed through in the company's telegraphic address, 'Litlangood'.

The Temperance movement

The emergence of the Temperance movement dates back to 1829 when the first anti-spirits group was formed in Greenock. Within ten years Temperance and Total Abstinence Societies had been established throughout Scotland. Their main effect was to reduce the number of licensed premises in towns and villages. At the same time, various forms of anti-drink organisations were established in the rest of Britain and Ireland and in the United States. They were most effective at times of economic recession, but it was not until the First World War that there was a real risk that the British Government would impose prohibition. The risk was greatest in the early months of 1915 when Lloyd George blamed the drink trade for the failure of the armaments industry to deliver sufficient guns and munitions urgently required at the front. In 1916 a new prohibitionist group, the Strength of Britain Movement, was formed, and its chief propagandist was the journalist Arthur Mee, who focused the movement's attack on the drink trade's use of scarce raw materials. DCL responded with press advertising and asked other distillers to help finance the formation of an anti-prohibition group. In May 1917 a Whisky Association was formed, based initially in London, to represent the interests of distillers, blenders and exporters. Within two years a fighting fund of over £100,000 had been raised and a new pressure group, the Freedom of Britain Movement, was formed. The threat of prohibition came again to the fore when the United States went dry in 1920. In Scotland the Temperance (Scotland) Act of 1913 allowed local voters to choose from three options: to vote for licences, to vote against licences or to limit the number of licences. Several areas selected to 'go dry'. In 1922 Wick in Caithness chose to have prohibition and it was effective until 1947. The Act was abolished in 1976.

with an agreement that no whisky would be sold until it had been matured for a minimum period of two years. A year later, compulsory bonding of whisky was extended to three years.

In April 1917, whisky companies were restricted to release for sale no more whisky than half the releases made in 1916. Barley and grain supplies needed by the whisky industry became increasingly in short supply, and in June 1917 all pot distilling was banned. The 1918 Budget doubled the rate of duty and the flat-rate price of a bottle of whisky was fixed at 9s (45p). Consumption fell to levels not experienced for nearly 100 years. In March 1919 the ban on pot still distilling was lifted and permission was given to increase stocks available for the home market to three-quarters of the 1916 releases. The agony of the whisky industry was further compounded with another huge

increase in duty from £1 10s (£1.50p) to £2 10s (£2.50p) per proof gallon. The distillers, blenders and merchants were only allowed to pass on half of this increase to their customers. The fixed price of a bottle of whisky was raised to 10s 6d (52.5p), compared with the retail price of 3s 6d (17.5p) in 1914.

There was yet again a large increase in duty in Austen Chamberlain's second Budget in 1920. This time the increase was £1 2s 6d (£1.12p) to £3 12s 6d (£3.62p) a proof gallon and the flat-rate price was again raised only by about one-half of the increase in duty to 12s 6d (62.5p) a bottle. Prices remained the same after the wartime Central Board of Control was disbanded in November 1921.

After the duty increase in 1920 there was to be a nineteen year gap before the level of duty was to be raised again.

PUNCH, OR THE LONDON CHARIVARI.—February 13, 1924.

"Any advantage as regards increased expectation of life lies with the moderate drinkers rather than with the total abstainers"

PROFESSOR RAYMOND PEARL
Professor of Vital Statistics, School of Hygiene & Public Health, John Hopkins University, Baltimore U.S.A.

FOR many years it has been the fashion for kill-joys, for politicians in distress, for persons with super-consciences who know little more of the world than a cat knows of a catechism, to think and to say that stimulants are made to lure the unwary to destruction.

Our outstandingly clever medical men (Prof. Ernest H. Starling, Dr. Robert Hutchison, Sir Frederick A. Mott, Prof. Raymond Pearl, etc., etc.) are speaking and writing in terms of refutation

that should make it no longer necessary for persons to apologise for the moderate use of all the gifts of a wise Providence.

All things are good if used properly. All good things can become bad by excessive use.

Quality is all-important, especially in respect of what we eat and what we drink. The price should always be a secondary consideration. For this reason you should not begrudge the little extra that you are asked to pay for

King William IV
SCOTS WHISKY

American doctors are prescribing King William IV for medicinal purposes

JOHN GILLON & CO LTD LONDON & LEITH
Telephone: Avenue 5214 Telegrams: "Litlangud, Fen, London" Cables: "Litlangud, London"
Wm. Williamson: *Chairman & Managing Director*
Head Office : 45 Leadenhall Street London E C

PUNCH, OR THE LONDON CHARIVARI.—February 25, 1925.

It is very cheering to me to know that so many of you are taking notice of my remarks and, instead of calling for "a Whisky and soda," saying instead "A Sandy Mac, please."

Sandy Macdonald
SCOTCH WHISKY

is one of the Whiskies that can safely be taken with soda *or with plain water.* Soda-water is necessary to cover the nakedness of some of the Whiskies that are being offered to you. They couldn't stand up by themselves. They need a splashing fountain to help them.
"Sandy Mac" is a safe Whisky. Your Doctor will confirm this if you send him a bottle.

MACDONALD, GREENLEES & WILLIAMS
(Distillers) LTD.
Leith – London – Aberdeen

(far left) 1924.

(left) 1925. Owned by Macdonald, Greenlees & Williams, *Sandy Macdonald* (chapter 9) regards itself as a safe whisky and that 'Your doctor will confirm this if you send him a bottle'!

The British economy slipped into a decade of depression, and in early 1920 the United States went 'dry'. This period of Prohibition lasted until repealed in 1933, but by then the production side of the whisky industry had deteriorated to such an extent that there were only a handful of malt whisky distilleries in production in the mid-1930s. The economy slowly recovered in the years immediately after the Great Depression, but the outbreak of war in 1939 dashed all hopes of any benefit that may have been enjoyed by the Scotch whisky industry.

At the beginning of the war the price of a bottle of whisky remained at the 1920 level: 12*s* 6*d* (62.5p) . By 1943 four increases in excise duty had doubled the bottle price to 25*s* 9*d* (a little over £1.25p) . With the need to improve dollar earnings, the industry was encouraged to concentrate on export and to restrict sales within the domestic market. In

March 1940 the Government imposed a cut of one-third in the production of malt whisky based on 1939 levels, and sales to home trade customers were cut by a fifth. In the following year domestic sales were further restricted to half the level of 1939 sales. The Government, having initially rationed supplies of barley for distilling purposes, decided that there would be no further distilling, and by October 1942 all distilleries were closed. It was to be a full two years later, towards the end of 1944, that a limited supply of about 100,000 tons of barley was again made available for distilling on condition that more of the industry's stocks of mature whiskies would be made available for export. Thirty-four malt distilleries opened in the first few months of 1945, and in April a further stimulus was given to the industry in Churchill's famous minute, 'On no account reduce the barley for whisky. This takes years

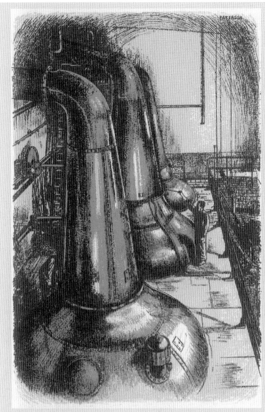

Malt, grain and blended Scotch whisky

Most of the examples of advertising discussed and illustrated in this book are of brands of blended Scotch whisky – that is whiskies that are a mixture of single malt and grain whiskies distilled and matured in Scotland. Using only malted barley in the pot still process, single malt Scotch whisky can only be the product of the one distillery where it is produced As with all Scotch whisky, it must be matured in oak casks in Scotland for a minimum of three years. This has been a legal requirement since 1916.

The second style of whisky distilled in Scotland is grain whisky, made from malted barley and other unmalted cereals in a Coffey or patent still in a process that is both continuous and highly efficient. The first patent still used to make grain whisky was developed by Robert Stein in 1826, but this was superseded four years later by the invention of an Irishman, Aeneas Coffey, who patented a superior version that was soon in widespread use.

Neil Gunn, in his classic book *Whisky and Scotland*, published in 1935, describes a patent still that produces the 'silent spirit' as it was once known, as 'an affair of two tall columns, heated by steam, into which wash is poured at one end and out of which pure alcohol pours at the other'.

Approximately nineteen out of every twenty bottles of Scotch whisky consumed throughout the world are bottles of blended whisky. There are many brands of blended whisky and there is a long list of those that have enjoyed success, with at least five of the largest global brands to survive the extraordinary trading conditions of the whole of the twentieth century portrayed in this book. The Master Blender of each blended whisky aims for long-term consistency, and single grain whiskies are chosen with the same care as the single malts that are put together to produce the final blend. Most blends are made up of at least thirty different single malts and several grain whiskies. The combination of malts and grains is usually a closely guarded secret and the proportion of malts to grains is rarely divulged, but is generally taken to be in the ratio of one-third single malt whiskies to two-thirds grains. Some of the more expensive premium blended Scotch whiskies can be expected to have been blended with a higher malt to grain ratio.

Alcoholic strength of Scotch whisky

From the early nineteenth century until 1980, when an international standard of measuring alcoholic strength was adopted in Britain and the rest of the European Community, the strength of spirits was measured in degrees. This, the Sykes system of measurement based on the use of the Bartholomew Sykes hydrometer, measured proof strength in degrees, starting with proof itself at 100° and absolute alcohol at 175°. Proof spirit was: 'a mixture of spirit and water of a strength of 57.1 per cent spirit by volume and 42.9 per cent water'.

The label on a pre-1980 standard bottle of Scotch whisky indicating 30° below strength – or 70° proof – has been replaced after 1980 with the information that the spirit is 40 per cent vol. (abv – alcohol by volume) .

Pot stills in a malt whisky distillery. Illustration courtesy of the Scotch Whisky Association

to mature and is an invaluable export and dollar producer.' After the war, it would be four years before production of malt whisky had returned to the pre-war level. In that year of 1949, the first malt whisky distillery to have been built for almost fifty years, Tullibardine distillery in Perthshire, entered production. It took until December 1953 before the Government ended its direct control of the production levels of the Scotch whisky industry, and a further six years before stocks of maturing whisky were in line with demand, and only then could rationing by means of a quota system be discontinued.

More distilleries came back into production, and during the 1950s the developing global demand for whisky stimulated a number of distillery owners to re-equip and expand their production.

Successive Governments further raised the level of excise duty on a bottle of whisky. The increase imposed by Selwyn Lloyd in the 1961 Budget raised the price of a standard blended whisky to 37s 6d (£1.87p) . The growth in demand continued apace during the 1960s, and DCL embarked on a programme of expansion increasing by half the number of stills in their distilleries. Over the same period malt whisky production soared from 16 million to over 50 million gallons and the demand for 'Scotch' in the American market trebled.

The early years of the 1970s saw the boom continue, and 1974 was to be the peak year of production. The global economy suffered as a result of the oil crisis in the mid-1970s, and for a few years so did the whisky industry.

Chapter 2
The Distillers Company Limited

(*previous page*) 1886. John Haig's Cameron Bridge distillery at Windygates in Fifeshire. The distillery was bought by John Haig in 1824, transferred to DCL in 1877 and is still in production.

The five other founder members of DCL in 1877 were: Robert Moubray – owning Cambus distillery at Alloa; D. Macfarlane & Co. – Port Dundas near Glasgow; Stewart & Co. – Kirkliston in West Lothian and Saucel at Paisley; McNab Bros & Co. – Glenochil near Stirling; John Bald & Co. – Carsebridge at Alloa.

In 1856, in an atmosphere of intense competition between Lowland grain distillers and falling profit margins, six of the largest companies entered into an arrangement known as the First Trade Agreement. It aimed to control production of the member companies and to regulate prices, sales volumes, discounts and credit arrangements. The group did not achieve its objectives and the agreement lasted only one year. Nine years after the first attempt to form the group, John Haig of Cameron Bridge distillery set about resurrecting the principles behind the original agreement. With the owner of Port Dundas, Scotland's largest grain distillery, replacing one of the members of the original group of six distillers who had gone out of business, the Scotch Distillers' Association was formed. Over the ensuing twelve years there were a few changes in membership but the group was not strong enough to withstand the intense competition between grain distillers in Scotland, England and Ireland, and from the increasing annoyance of competitively priced grain spirit imported from Germany.

In April 1877, five members of the Scotch Distillers' Association and one other, J Stewart & Co., owner of two grain distilleries, decided to form themselves into The Distillers Company Limited (DCL) , a Limited Liability Company with its head office in Edinburgh. In 1880 DCL sought a Stock Exchange quotation. The response from the public to acquire shares was slow, and this was not fully achieved until 1886. One of the original members of the 1856 Agreement, Menzies, Bernard & Craig, owners of the Caledonian distillery in Edinburgh, joined DCL in 1885.

The appointment in 1889 of William Ross as company secretary and accountant to the board of DCL was to mark a point in DCL's history, from which there would be the rapid development and diversification of the company. In 1894 DCL took its first step into the business of distilling malt whisky by building Knockdhu distillery to fulfill a contractual obligation to supply whisky to John Haig. Ross became DCL's general manager in 1897, and its managing director in 1900. DCL acquired five grain distilleries between 1902 and 1910; three were in Scotland and two in England. It was during this period that the company also developed its share of distilling in Ireland. Having acquired the Phoenix Park pot still distillery in Dublin in 1878, DCL took a fifty per cent interest in United Distillers, Ireland's largest grain whisky distiller.

In 1885 DCL had taken the decision to blend and bottle whisky for export. An export branch with blending, bottling and warehousing facilities was established at South Queensferry to the west of Edinburgh, in the shadow of the famous Forth Railway Bridge which was under construction at the time. Its brands of blended whisky, which included '*King George IV' Liqueur Whisky* and '*DCL' Very Old Special Scotch Whisky*, were registered between 1880 and 1890. The company's first attempts at export were generally unsuccessful due to a lack of commitment and constrained by fear of unfavourable reaction from

1911. The quality description 'liqueur' applied to whisky had been in use from the early years of the twentieth century. For example, *John Haig Gold Label* and *VAT 69* were routinely described and advertised as *Liqueur Scotch whiskies*. The Scotch Whisky Association (SWA) , established in 1917 to act on behalf of the whisky trade to protect the image and collective interests and integrity of Scotch whisky throughout the world, issued in 1949 a circular to its members recommending the removal of the word 'liqueur' from labels and advertisements. This action was taken to avoid any confusion between Scotch whiskies and those alcoholic liquors generally termed 'liqueurs'.

For Export only

"King George IV" LIQUEUR WHISKY.

"D.C.L." Very Old Special SCOTCH WHISKY.

Proprietors:
The Distillers Company Limited, Edinburgh.
(Capital Employed over £3,000,000 Sterling.)

Sole Distillers and Blenders of these and other brands of Whiskies well known and popular in Australia, Canada, India, South Africa, and throughout the World.

the wholesale trade. At the turn of the century and with a marked decline in sales in the home trade, the export effort was stepped up, and this proved to be successful. In 1916 DCL became firmly committed to the business of exporting when it bought two blended whisky companies, both with substantial and established export sales: John Hopkins & Co. Ltd and John Begg & Co. Ltd.

By 1910 James Buchanan & Co., John Dewar & Sons and John Walker & Sons had emerged as three of the largest distilling and blending companies, and had became known in the industry as the 'Big Three'. Over the period of the next fifteen years there were many discussions between these three companies and DCL, regarding a possible merger. In 1915 two of the 'Big Three', Buchanan and Dewar, merged to form Scotch Whisky Brands Ltd, and in 1919 the company was re-named Buchanan-Dewar Ltd. After more discussions and much wrangling over the terms of a merger, the 'Big Three' finally amalgamated with DCL in 1925, in what was known in the industry as 'The Big Amalgamation'.

Following the liquidation in 1914 of St Magdalene distillery to the west of Edinburgh, DCL, along with the owners of four Lowland pot still distilleries, Glenkinchie, Rosebank, Grange and Clydesdale, established a new company, Scottish Malt Distillers. The company known henceforth as SMD acquired two Highland malt distilleries, Glenlossie in 1919 and North Port in Brechin in 1922, and the group merged into DCL in 1925. As a result of these two very significant mergers DCL, in addition to its near absolute control of grain distilling, controlled thirty-two malt distilleries, and by 1935 this number had grown to fifty-one. In 1930 SMD was given the responsibility of controlling all of DCL's malt distilleries.

During the First World War and in the inter-war years the combined effects of wartime restrictions, Prohibition in the United States and a major period of economic recession put many companies into financial difficulty and risk of collapse. DCL took the opportunity to buy a number of distressed companies for their distilleries, whisky stocks and export-led brands of blended whisky. There were many acquisitions; the most significant were as follows:

The Times of India Annual, 1923.

THE "TOP NOTCH" OF SCOTCH

"King George IV" Whisky

"Say WHEN, Man!!"

"NOT A HEADACHE IN A HOGSHEAD"

Composed of the finest Highland Malt and Scotch Grain Whiskies from some of the most famous Distilleries in Scotland – now owned by the proprietors of this brand.

"King George IV." has set the fashion!

1923. A humorous illustration by Lawson Wood in *The Times of India Annual* goes much further than the *Cambus* advertisement of 1906: 'Not a headache in a hogshead'. A hogshead cask contains 65 gallons!

1916 DCL and the 'Big Three' acquired Dailuaine-Talisker Distilleries Co. Ltd, its whisky stocks and the company's three distilleries, Dailuaine, Imperial and Talisker.

1917 J & G Stewart Ltd of Edinburgh was acquired with its brands and 800,000 gallons (8,000 butts) of whisky for £2.3 million.

1919 Andrew Usher & Co. of Edinburgh and John Haig & Co. of Markinch.

1922 James Calder & Co. Ltd (the grain distilling company) and the Distillers Finance Corporation,

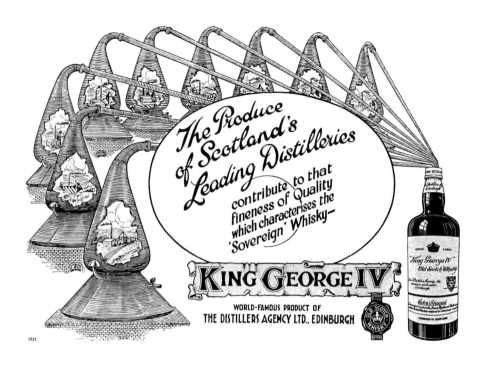

1932. By this date, DCL, through its subsidiary Scottish Malt Distillers, owned nearly fifty distilleries and accounted for over half the production of malt whisky in Scotland.

the Irish company owning most of Ireland's grain distilling capacity.

1922 The other branch of the Haig family, Haig & Haig Ltd, had been established in 1888 by John Alicius Haig, the brother of Hugh Veitch Haig, to market whisky in the United States. Before Prohibition, *Haig & Haig* had become a leading brand in the US. The Glasgow whisky blending firm of Robertson & Baxter had controlled Haig & Haig from 1907. In December 1922, following the voluntary liquidation of Robertson & Baxter, DCL and the 'Big Three' bought the company's stock of 2 million gallons of whisky and brands including *Haig & Haig Five Stars Scots Whisky*. DCL wanted to suppress *Haig & Haig* because its presence conflicted with the development of *John Haig*. For the purposes of bootlegging and rather than having to develop a new brand, the 'Big Three' wanted to revive *Haig & Haig* and capitalise on the value of the brand and

its heavy advertising in the past. This argument won the day and in 1925 Haig & Haig Ltd and its celebrated and unique decanter-shaped brand was made a subsidiary of John Haig.

1923 James Watson & Co. Ltd of Dundee with its main brand, *Watson's No.10* (which sold well in Australia) , and its stock of 5.5 million gallons of whisky was offered to DCL but, after a period of wrangling over the future of *No.10*, the company was acquired not by DCL, but by the 'Big Three'.

1924 When DCL was engaged in the discussions to merge its interests with those of the 'Big Three', it decided to cease conducting its export business under its own name and formed a subsidiary company, The Distillers Agency Ltd, to take over the business of its export branch.

1925 The 'Big Three' (James Buchanan & Co., John Dewar & Sons and John Walker & Sons) amalgamated with DCL.

1925 Peter Dawson Ltd, the Glasgow firm of distillers and blenders was acquired. DCL took full control of Sir James Calder's company, Macdonald Greenlees & Williams, and its three malt whisky distilleries, Auchinblae, Glendullan and Stronachie.

1927 Three years after his death, Peter Mackie's White Horse Distillers joined DCL.

1927 Bulloch Lade & Co. Ltd and its subsidiary Wright & Greig Ltd.

1928 Glasgow blenders, Benmore Distilleries Ltd and its four distilleries, including Dallas Dhu.

1957.

1933 Teaninich and Linkwood distilleries and Glasgow blenders, Macleay, Duff & Co. Ltd.

1935 The Glasgow firm of whisky wholesalers, Baird-Taylor Bros Ltd.

1936 Donald Fisher Ltd, Edinbugh-based blenders and exporters.

1937 Leith blenders, D & J McCallum Ltd and Booth's Distilleries Ltd, (owners of Wm Sanderson & Son Ltd, blenders of *VAT 69*) .

During and after the Second World War, DCL continued to make acquisitions. Leith-based whisky blenders and merchants, A & A Crawford Ltd, were taken over in 1944, and then in 1947 Gilmour Thomson & Co. Ltd and J & W Hardie Ltd were purchased. In 1954, following the cessation of trading by National Distillers of America, DCL acquired four distilleries: Glenury in Stonehaven, Glen Esk in Montrose, Benromach in Forres and Glenlochy in Fort William.

In 1986, the giant Irish brewing firm of Guinness, having the previous year bought the Perth-based whisky distillers and blenders Arthur Bell & Sons, took over DCL. Eleven years later, Guinness merged with Grand Metropolitan to create Diageo plc, the largest owner of distilleries in Scotland and the largest drinks company in the world. In order to satisfy the competition authorities in the United States, the new conglomerate sold its subsidiary company, John Dewar & Sons Ltd, and four distilleries to the Bacardi Corporation. Diageo plc currently operates twenty-seven malt distilleries and owns many of the world's leading brands of blended Scotch whisky.

A Luncheon Engagement · · · · · · · · · · · · · · · *from the original by Ernest Uden*

THE AGE OF ELEGANCE . . .

A knowledge and love of horses was one of the hallmarks of Britain in the early nineteenth century. To 'handle the ribbons', and to recognise 'a bit of blood' was part of the training of every young man about town. Today, judges of good horseflesh still abound, and of good Scotch Whisky too; they recognise a blend with the qualities of good breeding coupled with all the mature elegance of age . . .

OLD SCOTCH WHISKY

THE   DISTILLERS   AGENCY   LIMITED   EDINBURGH   SCOTLAND

Chapter 3
Advertising Scotch Whisky

The formation of Diageo plc in 1997 brought together a very fine portfolio of blended Scotch whisky brands. The long list includes several that have enjoyed enduring success, including the world's largest brand, *Johnnie Walker*, and other globally successful brands such as *J&B Rare, Haig, Black & White, VAT 69* and *White Horse*. Each brand has the remarkable distinction of being at least 100 years old!

Using material from the vast selection of advertising painstakingly put together by the company's team of archivists, *Still Going Strong* concentrates on the development of advertising of five historically important brands in the first sixty years of the last century. The final chapter is devoted to a collection of smaller brands that are either available in a few countries around the world or were consigned to history following their acquisition by DCL in the early part of the twentieth century. *J&B Rare* and *Bell's* are two brands that are very important to Diageo but with little in the way of archive material for the period covered by *Still Going Strong*, they have been excluded.

The main purpose of advertising is to create and develop brand awareness leading to an increase in the number of people trying the brand, hopefully liking it and then buying it on a regular basis. Each brand of blended Scotch whisky profiled in *Still Going Strong* began life at different times in the latter part of the nineteenth century, and sales developed at different rates. It was only after there had been some level of local and regional success in achieving firm support for the brand that the brand owner would deem it time to dip his toe into the advertising arena. At first, small advertisements were placed in local and regional newspapers and these were often supported with poster advertising. As the brand grew in popularity, offices were opened in London and larger provincial towns to serve the company's interests across the country. Operating out of each office would be a small team of sales representatives and the means of delivering whisky to the customers. When the brand became available across the country, the right conditions were in place to commence advertising in nationally available weekly and monthly newspapers and magazines.

The first advertisements of individual brands of Scotch whisky in nationally distributed newspapers and magazines appeared in the last few years of the nineteenth century. To support the sales effort behind the brands a wide range was developed of what is known today as point-of-sale material. These items were usually of a high quality and were designed to be useful and to provide strong visual reminders of the brand name. They were given away by the brand owner's representatives and included glass whisky dispensers, enamel signs, ashtrays, glass decanters, large mirrors for use in licensed premises, water jugs, serving trays, calendars, packs of playing cards, figurines, corkscrews, showcards and postcards. This was all at a time when there were no other forms of media such as radio, television or cinema to convey the whisky owner's advertising messages to the public.

As demand and sales of blended Scotch whiskies grew, by coincidence so did the range and number of magazines where advertisements could be placed. Two great advertising publications had been available since the 1840s; *The Illustrated London News* and *Punch* were respectively *the* illustrated newspaper and *the* magazine widely read by the opinion-formers of the late Victorian era and were for many years at the heart of the advertising schedules of the leading brands of Scotch whisky.

The world's first illustrated newspaper was *The Illustrated London News*, published by Herbert Ingram, a bookseller, newsagent and printer in premises on The Strand in London, on 14 May 1842. It was an immediate success: 26,000 copies of the first edition were sold, and by 1851, the year of The Great Exhibition in Hyde Park, sales had reached 130,000 per week. The first use of colour was in the Christmas edition of 1856. During the last two decades of the 1800s, advertisements became more prominent and were a welcome source of revenue for *The Illustrated London News* incurring enormous production costs in meeting its enlarged circulation. In the 1870s a typical issue contained two pages of advertisements at the end of the paper, and by the mid-1880s this had increased to six pages spread throughout the paper. Shortly after the turn of the century it was common for a single product to take up a whole page advertisement.

The Illustrated London News remained a weekly publication until 1971, when it was published monthly. Between 1989 and 1994 it was published bi-monthly, and since then it has been published twice a year, in summer and at Christmas.

Punch, or the *London Charivari*, was first published in July 1841. This illustrated magazine combining humour and political comment was the idea of Mark Lemon and Henry Mayhew. It was a strongly radical journal and its subtitle, *Charivari*, acknowledged as its model the radical Parisian magazine first published in 1831 by Philippon. During its first year of publication *Punch* sold 6,000 copies a week, but sales of least 10,000 were needed to cover costs. In December 1842 the financial difficulties that had developed led to the acquisition of *Punch* by Bradbury & Evans, a firm of printers and publishers.

Punch had a long and successful history but during the 1980s its circulation dropped dramatically, and the magazine closed in 1992. Mohammed Al Fayed re-launched the title in 1996 but it was again unsuccessful and publication ceased in June 2002.

Other publications favoured by brand owners and their agents were *The Graphic* (1869-1932) , *The Illustrated Sporting and Dramatic News* (1874-1943) , *The Bystander* (1903-1940) , *The Sketch* (1893-1959) , *The Sphere, Pears Annual* (1891-1926) , *The Tatler* (1901-1965, 1968-present day) , *Country Life* and *The Field*.

During the early decades of the twentieth century a few brand owners used advertisements to protest against political and social issues threatening the whisky industry. These ranged from the problems of defining 'What is Whisky?' to issues raised by government control of the industry during wartime. *Haig & Haig* argued against the soaring levels of excise duty, rationing and government control of retail price, and others took the opportunity to counter the growing threat of the Temperance movement and issues raised by Prohibition in the United States.

Many of the artists whose work appears in *Still Going Strong* were well known in their day producing artwork for posters, illustrations for books and postcards and designs for wallpaper and ceramics. Work by artists featured whose reputations continue to this day include Cecil Aldin, Heath Robinson, Arthur Wardle, Frank Reynolds, John Hassall,

Christopher Clark, Sir Bernard Partridge, Fougasse, Frank Mason and Clive Uptton. There were a few artists who were retained by brand owners for a number of years. *Johnnie Walker* used the work of Leo Cheney for the whole of the period between 1914 and 1927, and *Haig* and *Black & White* used Christopher Clark's work on various occasions over a similar length of time between 1922 and 1936.

Improvements in printing techniques and processes encouraged the whisky companies to advertise in colour but because of higher production costs and advertising charges, colour advertisements were generally used sparingly and for maximum impact in special editions and during the weeks leading up to Christmas. *Black & White* was the first brand to use colour in *The Bystander* in 1912. *Haig's* first colour advertisement was in 1924, followed by *Johnnie Walker's* extensive use of colour in the period 1927 to 1930, and *White Horse's* first colour advertisement appeared in 1928.

From the earliest days of advertising whisky brand owners have sought to assure customers that their brands have a consistent quality. It is a recurring theme, sometimes in a small strap line supporting the main copy line or as the main subject of an advertisement. As brands grew in popularity the owners wished to assure their customers that there were adequate stocks of maturing whisky to support current and future sales, without the risk of compromising quality.

In the period leading up the Second World War there was a subtle development in advertising to reflect the changes in social behaviour. Leisure activities were increasingly portrayed, such as dining in restaurants, attending sports events or partaking in sporting activities. In 1926 *Johnnie Walker* launched the Hole-in-One award, offering a bottle of their whisky to any golfer claiming this special achievement. Aimed at a particular section of the brand's target market, it developed into a very successful extension of traditional advertising in Britain and many of the company's export markets.

The early 1930s saw the first and somewhat brief use of photographic subjects in magazine advertising. Artist-drawn subjects were soon to return and were not to be replaced as the main advertising style until the 1960s.

During the Second World War there was a general decline in advertising and reduction in print quality although *Johnnie Walker* produced an interesting campaign in colour in support of the war effort at home, under the banner of 'Good work... good whisky'.

In the fifteen years or so after the end of the war advertising became somewhat erratic and fragmented in its style. It was probably marking time for the better years that were round the corner. Whisky was supplied to the home market on a quota basis until 1959, and whisky companies were concentrating on developing their export markets, especially to the United States and the 'old' empire. The steady improvements in living conditions in Britain during the 1960s were reflected in the increasing use of 'lifestyle' advertising.

And it is in the 1960s where *Still Going Strong* ends its look into whisky's advertising history. Brand owners were being offered a whole new raft of platforms to stimulate interest in attracting new users and keeping loyal brand support. The cinema, radio, large poster sites and eventually television were to become more attractive and flexible advertising media than the magazines and illustrated newspapers that had played such a prominent role in the successful development of so many brands of blended Scotch whisky.

Chapter 4
Johnnie Walker

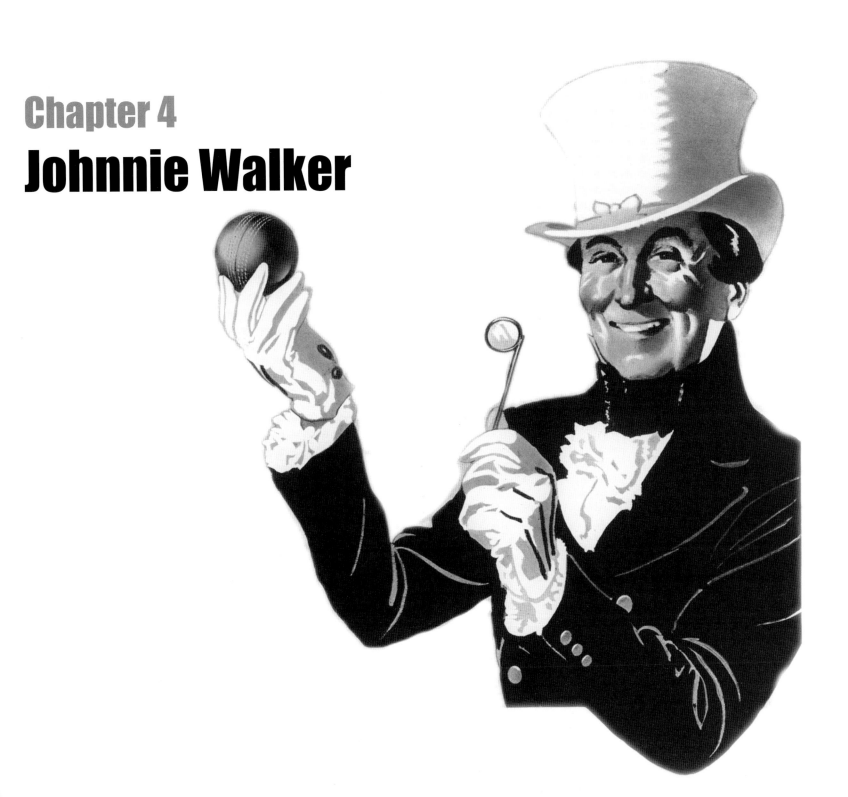

In 1820 the trustees of the estate of tenant farmer Alexander Walker decided that Alexander's son John, at the age of fifteen, was too young to run the farm. They purchased a small warehouse and a grocery and wine and spirit business in the Ayrshire town of Kilmarnock and placed John in charge of the business. At that time Kilmarnock was a thriving town where lace curtains, knitted woollen goods and carpets were manufactured. It was also an important centre of coal mining, and this led to the first railway in Scotland, laid down in 1812 to connect the town to the port of Troon to enable coal to be transported to the coast by means of horse traction.

Kilmarnock's importance was further enhanced when more railway connections were built through the town, connecting Glasgow to the north with Ayr, and Dumfries and Carlisle to the south.

In due course, when John Walker's son, Alexander, joined the business, the first move was made in the eventual creation of the Walker whisky empire when the family began to sell on a wholesaling basis their own '*Walker's Kilmarnock blended whiskies*'. John Walker died in 1857 and Alexander succeeded him as head of the business.

In 1860, three years after John's death, the firm's sales had reached 100,0000 gallons of whisky and interest was developing in Walker's whiskies in the London market.

With a change in the law to allow the blending of malt and grain whiskies under bond, Alexander developed a flourishing business in blended whisky, registering in 1867 the copyright to *Walker's Old Highland Whisky*. By the late 1870s Walker's whisky was being sold in the distinctive square bottle that is still in use today. Demand in England was such that in 1880 an office was opened in London.

Alexander brought his two sons, George Paterson and John, into the business in 1886, and in the same year the family firm became a private limited company. Two years later Alexander junior joined the firm and at that time Walkers were exporting to over seventy countries and with the expansion of business in south-east England the company moved to larger premises in London, with offices, bottling facilities and cellars.

Following Alexander's death in 1889, George succeeded him as chairman; a position he held until his retirement in 1923. The following year John Walker went to Australia and opened a sales office in Sydney. He successfully prepared the foundation for a huge demand for Walker's whiskies in that country but unfortunately his health deteriorated and he died in 1896.

Walker's whiskies won the highest awards at many exhibitions and competitions during the last two decades of the nineteenth century: Sydney in 1879, Melbourne in 1881, Paris in 1885, Adelaide in 1887, Dunedin in 1890,

An early twentieth-century advertisement drawn by W. Heath Robinson

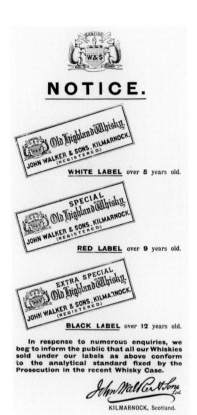

(left) 1906. Walker's Kilmarnock Old Highland Whisky was available at three different ages. The standard *White Label* was a blend over five years old. The *Red Label* blend, known as the *Special Old Highland Whisky*, was over nine years old and the top of the range *Black Label*, at over twelve years old, was labelled *Extra Special Old Highland whisky*.

(left) 1906. One of the first advertisements to depict Walker's unique square-shaped bottle came with assurances that the company had the largest maturing stocks of pure malt Scotch whisky of quality, age and uniformity.

The Tatler. 2 December 1908. This is the first example of the use in national advertising of Tom Browne's Johnnie Walker 'Striding Man' that was to feature in this guise in advertising for the next fifty or so years. *Walker's Kilmarnock Whiskies* have now clearly been re-named *Johnnie Walker Whisky* and another first is the appearance of the slogan 'Born 1820… Still going strong'. In the copy there is a further assurance on the subject of quality that the company has a stock of 3.5 million gallons of pure malt Scotch whisky and there has also been a small increase in the minimum age of two whiskies in the range. The *White Label* is over six years old and the *Red Label* is over ten years old.

Jamaica in 1891, Kimberley in 1892 and Brisbane in 1897. By the end of the 1890s the firm had appointed agents in New Zealand and South Africa.

To support the rapidly growing sales of the company's blends there was a need to guarantee the supply of high quality Speyside malt whisky and thus the move was made in 1893 to buy Cardow distillery, Walker's main source of malt whisky. In 1897 the company opened an office in Birmingham, managed by James Stevenson who had joined the company in 1890 as a junior member of the office staff.

The need to handle the increasing volume of business necessitated expansion of the Kilmarnock premises. Rather than build new premises the company acquired in 1899 a share in the business of Slater Rodger & Co. Ltd, a Glasgow based firm of whisky blenders and

owners of Banff distillery. The Kilmarnock premises were retained and the move gave Walkers large warehouse accommodation with blending and bottling facilities and a railway siding to expedite the distribution of whisky. Three years later larger premises were again needed in London, and St George's bonded warehouse with bottling facilities was constructed in Commercial Road, and in 1907 further growth of sales in England led to the opening of an office in Manchester.

In 1908 James Stevenson moved from Birmingham to take over the London office. During the First World War Stevenson was co-opted by Lloyd George to coordinate the Ministry of Munitions and along with Peter Mackie, chairman of *White Horse* whisky, successfully countered the proposal for the total abolition of alcohol. For his work during the war, Stevenson received a baronetcy in

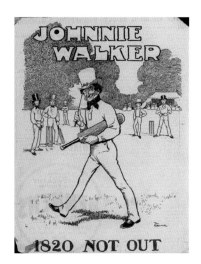

(above) 1909. Tom Browne drew a series of sporting scenes that were used in advertisements and promotional material for many years. Johnnie Walker is, as will so often be the case, in a confident assured mood, and more often than not depicted moving from right to left.

(above right) 1910. After its appearances in 1908 the *Johnnie Walker* whisky bottle rarely featured in advertising until the early 1930s, although it makes a brief reappearance in 1915 and again in 1925. Following the conclusion of the 'What is whisky?' controversy, the company incorporated on the bottom label of the bottle a statement assuring the drinkers of *Johnnie Walker* that it is 'Guaranteed same quality throughout the world'.

(right) 1910.

1917, and this was followed by a peerage in 1924. He was chairman of the board that organised the British Empire Exhibition at Wembley in 1924 and 1925, and died the following year, aged fifty-three.

In 1908 Alexander Walker gave Tom Browne, a famous cartoonist and commercial artist of that time, a portrait of the company's founder, John Walker, and asked him to use it to create a subject suitable for the company's trade mark and for use on labels and in advertising. The result was the striding character of 'Johnnie Walker' and the *Kilmarnock* range of whiskies was renamed *Johnnie Walker*.

John Walker & Sons Ltd continued to expand at a pace. Agents were appointed in Paris in 1910, and Burma and Egypt in 1911. It was at this time that Walkers was in discussion with the two whisky companies of John Dewar and James Buchanan, with a view to amalgamation. Known in the industry as the 'Big Three', they could not agree terms for a merger. In 1911 the company took a controlling interest in Slater Rodger & Co. Ltd and bought the Kilmarnock firm of whisky blenders, William Wallace & Co., owners of the Real Mackay brand and the wholesale wine and spirit business of Malcolm Ferguson & Co. of Glasgow.

In 1912, along with DCL, Walkers acquired A&J Dawson, owners of St Magdalene distillery in Linlithgow, and again in 1916, with DCL, bought Clynelish distillery following the bankruptcy of James Ainslie & Co. of Leith. To ensure an adequate supply of bottles especially for the export market, Walkers bought a significant share of a bottle-making firm in Castleford, Yorkshire. This firm was later purchased outright and with the installation of automated bottling machinery and reserve stocks of bottles, the fear of shortage was removed.

Difficulties arose in a number of export markets where bottles that had contained *Johnnie Walker* whisky were re-filled with locally produced spirit. In a move to remedy this situation, a syndicate of bottle manufacturers developed a capsule fitment to replace the cork and make it impossible to re-fill the bottle. Walkers invested £5,000 to gain a one-third share of this group, the Anglo-American Patent Bottle

1910. Tom Browne's death had given Walkers a problem: how and who could continue the development of the advertising theme that he had originated? Bernard Partridge stepped into the breach with this Christmas 1910 subject successfully interpreting the style of Tom Browne.

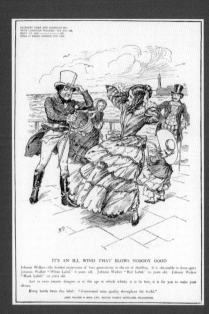

1911. Walkers was the first whisky company to produce several series of advertisements each with a common theme and a variety of interesting, entertaining, enlightening and gently amusing subjects. Bernard Partridge's 'Fashions come and Fashions go' took centre stage in *The Illustrated London News* in 1911.

1913. Leonard Raven Hill's second series: 'Old Songs'.

1912. Leonard Raven Hill was brought on board in 1912 to develop the style of Tom Browne's concept of the Johnnie Walker 'Striding Man'. He designed two delightful series: the first, in 1912 and running into 1913, was based on 'Old London Cries': 'Milk below, Maids – New milk from the cow!'.

1914. With Britain's involvement in the First World War in August 1914, *Johnnie Walker* was quickly off the mark to produce advertisements of a patriotic nature with recruitment the first priority. They were illustrated by Leo Cheney, who was to produce all *Johnnie Walker*'s magazine advertisements over the next thirteen years.

(above) 1914. Number 4 in the *Johnnie Walker* War Cartoon series illustrated by Leo Cheney. With words by Robert Burns, little is left to the imagination. The message is simple: militarism must be eradicated.

(above right) 1915. An example from a series featuring soldiers from Commonwealth countries.

(right) 1915. The first known advertisement to feature exclusively *Johnnie Walker Black Label. Johnnie Walker White Label* was discontinued in 1918.

Co. Ltd. This action was deemed necessary to safeguard Walker's reputation as stated on the label: 'Guaranteed same quality throughout the world'.

The Immature Spirits (Restrictions) Act of May 1915 made it compulsory to keep spirits in bond for two years: this was extended one year later to a minimum of three years. The price of single malt whiskies soared and Walkers found it necessary to restrict the sales of their whisky and to seek further stocks. In 1915, along with DCL they bought John Robertson & Son of Dundee and its Coleburn distillery near Elgin.

In 1916, in association with DCL, John Dewar & Sons and W.P. Lowrie (controlled from 1906 by James Buchanan & Co. Ltd) Walkers bought a quarter share in Dailuaine-Talisker Distilleries Ltd and its three distilleries, Dailuaine, Talisker and Imperial. Government restrictions on the making of whisky meant that Walkers were unable to fully meet the demand for their whiskies. More acquisitions were made after the war with the purchase in 1922, with Buchanan-Dewar and DCL, of 2 million gallons of whisky at the cost of over £1 million from Robertson & Baxter Ltd of Glasgow and the company, Haig & Haig Ltd.

Walkers became a public company in March 1923. Two months later, in conjunction with John Dewar & Sons Ltd

and W.P. Lowrie & Co. Ltd, they bought James Watson & Co. of Dundee, and divided the 8 million gallons of whisky stocks between the three firms, thus further easing the acute shortage. Walkers also acquired more whisky stocks in July 1923 when they bought one of Speyside's largest distilleries, Mortlach distillery in Dufftown, for £150,000. In spite of the various acquisitions of companies and whisky stocks, the demand for *Johnnie Walker* from the home and export markets was continuing to exceed supply and the company was forced in June 1923 to restrict sales to all markets for one year.

After many discussions about a possible merger of the 'Big Three' that began in 1909, Buchanan-Dewar and John Walker & Sons Ltd finally agreed on terms and amalgamated with DCL, in 1925, to form one of Britain's largest companies.

1920. Fiji. The war is over and it is time to remind the readers that *Johnnie Walker* is a truly international brand of Scotch whisky. The *Johnnie Walker* Travel Series was the first of Cheney's five post-war series of advertisements, each with between sixteen and thirty-six subjects.

1920 is also Walker's centenary year: 'From George the Third to George the Fifth. One hundred years long. Born 1820. Still going strong.'

1922. In the Historical Spirit Series an historical character is featured against a background of a famous hostelry or building. In this example, Dick Turpin is featured with the 'Spaniards Inn' in London's Hampstead Heath. This advertisement appeared in *The Illustrated London News* Wedding Number of 4 March 1922, issued to commemorate the wedding of Princess Mary, King George V's only daughter, to Viscount Lascelles.

1924. An example from the Literary Spirit Series features Ben Jonson enjoying the vaporous atmosphere of the 'Old Mermaid Tavern' in London's Aldergate Street.

1924 was a very special year for the company, with sales of *Johnnie Walker* whiskies in Britain exceeding one million cases for the first time.

1925. Fish-fly making is number 4 in Leo Cheney's Old Craft Series that ran between December 1924 and April 1926.

1925. There is perhaps more than a little irony in this advertisement appearing in the *Punch* Summer 1925 number a few weeks after John Walker & Sons Ltd lost its 'independence', having merged earlier that year with DCL.

1926. The humorous Old Sayings Series was the fifth and last of Leo Cheney's post-war contributions to *Johnnie Walker*'s advertising. He died in September 1928.

1926. The hugely successful *Johnnie Walker* Hole-in-One competition was launched in 1926, and was used for many years as a powerful promotional device in Britain and many countries around the world.

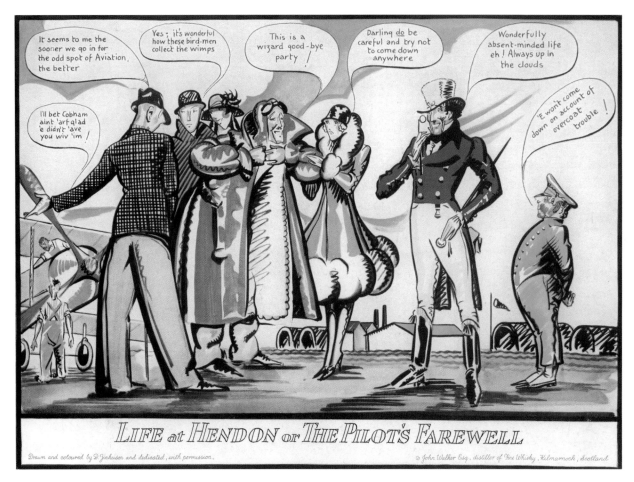

1927. Life at Hendon or the Pilot's Farewell. *Johnnie Walker*'s first use of colour advertising was in a series about life in London and it marked an extraordinary and bizarre departure from their hitherto traditional style of advertising. First seen in *Country Life* magazine, there are at least thirteen subjects in the series 'drawn and coloured' by theatrical sets and costumes designer Doris Zinkeisen.

1927. Piccadilly Up Again.

April 18, 1928   *The Sketch*   129

LET us consider hats in general.

There are hats that are talked about, hats that are talked through— thrown in the air, sworn by.

The hat, which is for one man the symbol of his sovereignty, is for another merely an article of diet, the indigestible penalty of a rash wager.

And let us consider *this* hat. Johnnie Walker's. The hat to which all the aforementioned are raised in token of a respect not unmingled with affection.

JOHNNIE WALKER

Born 1820—Still going Strong!

JOHN WALKER & SONS LTD., *Scotch Whisky Distillers* KILMARNOCK, SCOTLAND

1928. Twenty years after his creation by Tom Browne, the *Johnnie Walker* 'Striding Man' had become the advertising icon of what was becoming the largest selling brand of Scotch whisky in the world. In a six-month burst of advertising, *Johnnie Walker* gave the magazine readers of Britain a full explanation of the various items of clothing and accoutrements that *Johnnie Walker* wore and carried – firstly his hat.

Mar 12, 1928   THE ILLUSTRATED LONDON NEWS

INFINITE in their variety are the productions of 'the gentle craft.' Wellingtons, Bluchers, army boots, beetle crushers, boots with elastic sides, slippers with no sides at all, vegetarian sandals . . . .

And here are boots before which even the fabled Seven-league Boots must sing small. Johnnie Walker's, these —the famous Hessians that ring on every highway of the world.

Any man who seeks a better 'Scotch' than Johnnie Walker had best go barefoot. For his quest must inevitably be bootless.

JOHNNIE WALKER

Born 1820—Still going Strong

JOHN WALKER & SONS LTD, SCOTCH WHISKY DISTILLERS, KILMARNOCK, SCOTLAND.

1928. Boots.

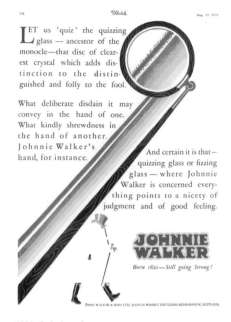

130   *The Sketch*   Aug 15, 1928

LET us 'quiz' the quizzing glass — ancestor of the monocle—that disc of clearest crystal which adds distinction to the distinguished and folly to the fool.

What deliberate disdain it may convey in the hand of one. What kindly shrewdness in the hand of another. Johnnie Walker's hand, for instance.

And certain it is that— quizzing glass or fizzing glass — where Johnnie Walker is concerned everything points to a nicety of judgment and of good feeling.

JOHNNIE WALKER

Born 1820 – Still going Strong!

JOHN WALKER & SONS LTD, SCOTCH WHISKY DISTILLERS, KILMARNOCK, SCOTLAND.

1928. Quizzing glass.

Oct. 13th, 1928.   COUNTRY LIFE.   xlix.

TURNING now to the handkerchief. Not exactly an article of attire, but a most necessary adjunct. Designed for humble uses, nevertheless it has its great moments. As when it is flourished frantically in victory, waved in welcome, or fluttered in farewell.

And *this* handkerchief — Johnnie Walker's — could it be lifted from the page, might well be dropped upon the shoulder as a mark of world-wide favour. Whose shoulder? His own.

JOHNNIE WALKER

Born 1820 – Still going Strong!

JOHN WALKER & SONS, LTD, SCOTCH WHISKY DISTILLERS, KILMARNOCK, SCOTLAND.

1928. Handkerchief.

The Sketch   Oct. 2, 1929

Born 1820 –   *Still going Strong*

JOHN WALKER AND SONS LIMITED, SCOTCH WHISKY DISTILLERS, KILMARNOCK, SCOTLAND.

1929. The complete Johnnie Walker.

1930. The sporting theme in advertising developed and in 1930 this rather contrived link between golf scores and the date when *Johnnie Walker* was established was one of a small series of advertisements each with sporting links.

1931. 'Buy British for Christmas'. This was the year Britain suffered from severe economic depression and high unemployment, and a national coalition government was formed to solve the crisis facing the country. One of the many steps taken was a campaign to encourage the nation to 'Buy British' and Fougasse's cartoon was suitably endorsed.

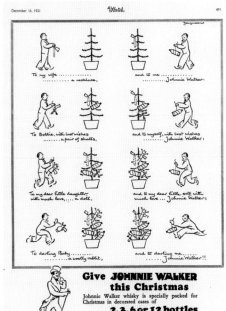

1929. The worldwide economic recession combined with competitive sales activity of other brands of Scotch whisky, notably *Black & White* and *Haig*, were having a negative effect on sales of *Johnnie Walker* in Britain. Sales steadily declined from the best year of 1926 until a 'low' was reached in 1950. It was then to take a further twenty-five years until sales reached the level achieved in 1926. Advertising *Johnnie Walker* continued but probably at a reduced rate of expenditure and, as will be seen on this and subsequent pages, the subjects and styles of advertising were routinely changed. Advertisements drawn twenty years earlier by Tom Browne were used in a small burst of advertising in 1929.

1931. This montage was the first by *Johnnie Walker* to employ photographic subjects.

1932. Appearing in *The Sketch* issue of 13 April, ten days before the FA Cup Final at Wembley where Newcastle United beat Arsenal 2-1.

1935.

1936. A cricket ball and poorly blended whiskies lead gently to *Johnnie Walker*'s special qualities and the suggestion that *Johnnie Walker* should be asked for by name.

1938. A neat advertising device to link the fashionable sport of cricket and *Johnnie Walker*'s traditional methods of whisky-making. The 'short holiday from distilling in the summer months' is delightfully known in the whisky industry as the 'silent' or 'off' season.

1938. Part of the continuing campaign to emphasise the steps taken to produce the quality whisky that is *Johnnie Walker*.

Gentlemen!
your **Johnnie Walker**—

In the stately homes of England, Johnnie Walker is very much at home. In the most distinguished circles this fine whisky takes its place, as to the Manor born. For there is an aristocracy among Scotch whiskies. And only the very finest of them—*all* the very finest of them—mellowed and matured by time and blended with traditional skill, are assembled in every bottle of Johnnie Walker.

Born 1820
—still going
strong

1939. Gentlemen had been, and still are, in 1939, the target of *Johnnie Walker*'s advertising. Which one of these two gentlemen will attempt to fill the glasses – and how?!

1940. 'Good work – good whisky' was Johnnie Walker's advertising campaign throughout the Second World War and into 1946. 'Dig for Victory' was the first subject.

Good work – good whisky

JOHNNIE WALKER

Born 1820—still going strong

1941. The telegram reads: 'Congratulations on completing well ahead of schedule date. Good work'. This is a rare sighting of a whisky advertisement with empty glasses.

1943. There are many walls and gardens in Britain that still bear the scars of the iron railings removed and melted down for re-use in the war effort.

1944. Marine artist Frank Mason depicts merchant vessels in convoy.

1946. The final subject in the series was illustrated by Rowland Hilder.

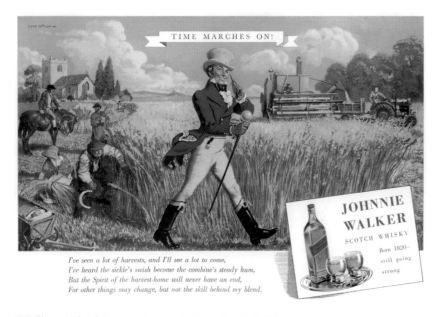

1948. The agricultural theme continues in the first subject in the 'Time marches on' series, illustrated by Clive Uptton.

1955. The artist is again Clive Uptton, and the subject is the elegance of the social scene.

1949. Artist: Clive Uptton.

1961. We have reached the stage in whisky advertising where lifestyle and the social scene take over, and here we have a small social group, a charming lady and her cigarette, a handsome man and a well-filled glass of *Johnnie Walker*, 'Born 1820 – still going strong'. This marks the end of this chapter charting the progress and development of *Johnnie Walker*'s advertising over a period of fifty-five years. *Johnnie Walker* was to go forward from strength to strength and quite simply it had become and, over forty years later, it still is, the world's favourite whisky.

Lamplight and Johnnie Walker. Glowing golden. Chuckling into glasses from the grand square bottle. Scotch of Scotch, yes, welcoming, mellow. At home or away – **Good old Johnnie Walker**

BORN 1820—still going strong

Chapter 5
Black & White

1929. In 1898 James Buchanan paid £87,000 to buy Anderson & Co.'s Black Swan distillery. The rebuilding scheme of such a valuable site fronting to Holborn called for an equally important and striking design of building, and this work was entrusted to Edward Martin FRIBA, a young and promising architect who subsequently designed many notable buildings in London. An article in the house magazine, *DCL Gazette*, in 1931, recalls that the architect 'was influenced by the romantic work of the continental architects of the fifteenth and sixteenth centuries, who, untrammelled by conventions and precedents, had created work of surpassing freedom and beauty'. Allen Andrews, in his book *The Whisky Barons*, was less than complimentary about the building, regarding it as 'a rather fanciful turreted creation of a style somewhere between Balmoral-baronial and Hans Christian Andersen'.

THE ILLUSTRATED LONDON NEWS CHRISTMAS NUMBER. 1929.—2

B orn in 1849 in the Canadian province of Ontario, James Buchanan, the youngest son of Scottish emigrant parents, was to become the founder of one of the most famous blended whiskies in the world, *Black & White*. Before his first birthday James and his family returned to Scotland and, because of his delicate health, he was educated privately until, at the age of fourteen, he began his business career as an office boy in a Glasgow shipping firm. After six years he joined his brother's grain merchant business and, after a further ten years, moved to London and acted as an agent for the whisky merchants Charles Mackinlay & Co. It was not until James Buchanan was thirty-five years old that he decided to establish his own business. He approached William Lowrie, chairman of

BUCHANAN
BLEND
SCOTCH WHISKY

JAMES BUCHANAN & CO.
SCOTCH WHISKY DISTILLERS.
By Appointment to
H.M. THE QUEEN
AND H.R.H.
THE PRINCE OF WALES.

1900. The first advertisement for *The Buchanan Blend* depicting the label and bottle shows that the whisky is supplied to the House of Commons and that the company has the Royal Warrant, first granted to them in 1898, to supply Queen Victoria and HRH the Prince of Wales.

THE POPULAR
SCOTCH
IS
"BLACK & WHITE"

JAMES BUCHANAN & CO.
SCOTCH WHISKY DISTILLERS.
By Appointment to
H.M. THE QUEEN
AND H.R.H.
THE PRINCE OF WALES.

1903. Deliveries from the Black Swan Distillery of *Black & White* and *Special Buchanan* (the new name for *Buchanan Blend*) were made in splendid horse-drawn vehicles. Engraving by Joseph Swain.

1905. This strongly royalist advertisement appeared several times during the reign of King Edward VII. *Special Buchanan* had again been renamed: *Special (Red Seal)* .

1900. It is not entirely clear if the whisky in *The Buchanan Blend* was the same as James Buchanan's choice of whisky in this black bottle with a white label that he specially selected and supplied to the House of Commons. From this advertisement it would appear that the whisky had no specific brand name to refer to other than *Buchanan*. James Buchanan had accepted that the public, when unable at the point of ordering the whisky to recall the name 'Buchanan', referred to it as 'that black and white whisky'. The brand name *Black & White* was emerging, and Buchanan incorporated the great whisky name of the future into this advertisement.

(above) 1906. First registered as a trade mark in 1904, the brand name *Black & White* is now on the label, albeit less prominent than House of Commons.

(right) 1908. One for the road – or perhaps the half a tumbler of *Black & White* is refreshment after a long journey!

(far right) 1908. Edwardian elegance and the presence of a woman in a man's world of whisky advertising marks the last appearance of a *Black & White* bottle in the company's advertising until 1925.

a successful Glasgow firm of whisky brokers and blenders, to borrow capital to start his business and obtain supplies of whiskies to produce his own blend. He became the sole proprietor of his new venture, James Buchanan & Co., which was first registered in 1884. Buchanan produced a blend of some older whiskies, creating a lightness of taste that he felt would be more appropriate to the English palate than the traditional heavy, strong tasting Highland and Lowland malt whiskies. *The Buchanan Blend of Fine Old Scotch Whiskies* was made up in casks in Glasgow and shipped to London to be sold in small casks to the licensed public houses in the city. His first year of trading was so successful that he was able to repay his loan to Lowrie. His enthusiasm and devoted salesmanship found

many new friends for his whisky. Buchanan decided to put some of his whisky in black glass bottles with a white label declaring the contents as: 'The Buchanan Blend of Fine Old Scotch Whiskies - suitable for Grog or Toddy'.

Within a year he had secured the supply of his Scotch whisky to the bars and cellars of the House of Commons. A letter from the catering contractors to the House of Commons praised the whisky, stating:

> The *Buchanan Blend* of Scotch Whisky you now supply to this Department is much liked by the Members and others who use it. It is with great pleasure that we express our high opinion of its quality.

BUCHANAN'S SCOTCH WHISKY

"BLACK & WHITE" BRAND.

BUCHANAN'S SCOTCH WHISKY

"BLACK & WHITE" BRAND.

(far left) 1910. Many different black and white subjects were to be used by Buchanans before the black and white terriers became an integral and essential part of the brand's advertising. Firstly there are Sealyham Terriers.

(left) 1910. The only surviving dog of Shackleton's expedition to the South Pole was this fine Husky. Artist: M Kirmse.

THE SPHERE

BUCHANAN'S
Scotch Whisky

A GRAND SPIRIT

"BLACK & WHITE" BRAND

The Bystander, May 1, 1912

BUCHANAN'S WHISKY

BUCHANAN'S "BLACK & WHITE" LEADS

"BLACK & WHITE" BRAND

Printed for the Proprietors, Messrs. H. R. Bacnes & Company, Ltd., by Messrs. W. H. Smith & Son, 55, Fetter Lane, London, E.C., and published weekly by Messrs. H. R. Bacnes & Company, Ltd., at Tallis House, Whitefriars, in the City of London.—May 1, 1912. Entered as second-class mail matter at New York (N.Y.) Post Office.

(far left) 1911. Newfoundland and Jack Russell. Artist: Maud Earl.

(left) 1912. Buchanan's *Black & White* Leads. The brand's first colour advertisement appeared in the 1 May edition of *The Bystander*. Artist: A.C.

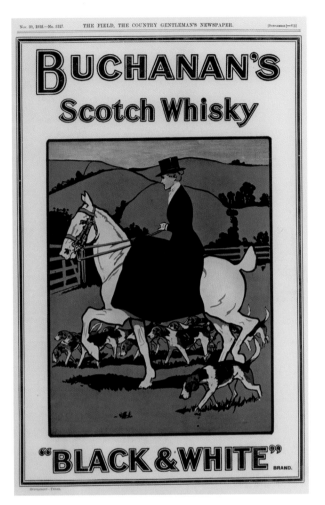

(above) 1912. 'Still Watchers' is the first known advertisement to feature the black and white dogs: the Scottish and West Highland Terriers.

(right) 1912. Artist: Unsigned, but likely to be Cecil Aldin.

(far right) 1912. 'A Morning Nip' by Maud Earl.

Two years later, in April 1888, Buchanan became the exclusive supplier of Scotch whisky to the House of Commons, and in the following year his blended whisky won the gold medal at the Paris Centennial Exhibition.

Buchanan's customers often referred to his whisky in the distinctive black bottle with its plain white label as Black and White. By the 1890s, through an enormous personal sales effort, Buchanan had firmly established the brand in London's clubs, hotels and music halls. To ensure a good supply of the right malt whisky for his blend, and in partnership with William Lowrie, he built Glentauchers distillery on Speyside and production began in May 1898.

With rapidly developing export success the company needed larger offices, and in the same year he bought Anderson & Co.'s Black Swan distillery in London's Holborn. Buchanan demolished the distillery and built his new headquarters on the site. The new premises consisted of five floors of spacious offices, with ample bottling, storage and loading facilities.

Regional sales offices were opened in Bristol and Birmingham in 1899, and two years later in Manchester. By 1902, the company's European sales were considerable and the first overseas office was opened in Paris in 1902 and later in the same year in New York.

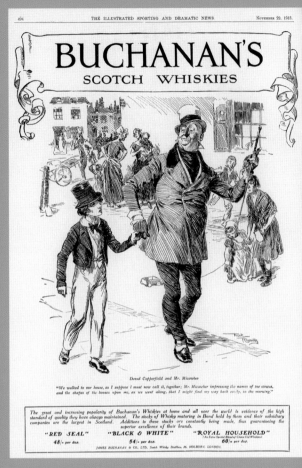

1915. 'Study in Black and White': one of a series of wartime naval subjects by Charles Pears.

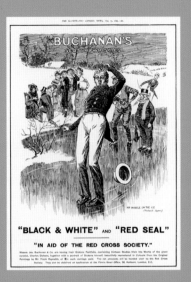

1915. Mr Winkle from Charles Dickens's *Pickwick Papers*. Artist: Frank Reynolds.

1913. A full-page drawing by Frank Reynolds of David Copperfield and Mr Micawber is one of a series by the artist to be used by *Black & White* during the period 1913 to 1928.

Red Seal is retailing at 48s a dozen (20p per bottle) , *Black & White* at 54s a dozen (22.5p per bottle) and a new premium priced brand, *Royal Household: An Extra Special Blend of Choice Old Whiskies* at 60s a dozen (25p per bottle) .

1915. Artist: Maud Earl.

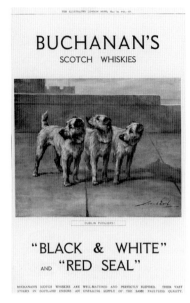

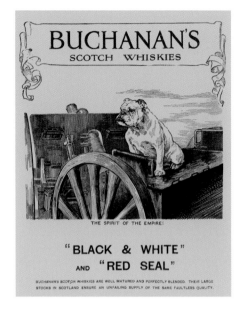

JAMES BUCHANAN & CO., LTD., SCOTCH WHISKY DISTILLERS, 26, HOLBORN, LONDON, E.C.

(above) 1915. Maud Earl captures the character of the Border Terrier in this study entitled 'Dublin Fusiliers'. Others in the series include 'Black Watch' and 'Yorkshire Light Infantry'.

(above right) 1916. The British Bulldog is used to good effect in 'The Spirit of the Empire'.

(right) 1916. Maud Earl's painting of a Pointer in the *Pears Christmas Annual* of 1916.

Buchanan converted James Buchanan & Co. into a limited liability company in 1903, retaining full ownership of the shares, and in the same year he acquired Bankier distillery in Stirlingshire. Three years later Buchanan bought the business of his ageing friend Lowrie, thus giving Buchanan full ownership of Glentauchers distillery and to add further distilling capacity he bought Convalmore distillery in Dufftown. He continued the expansion of his business by building a new bonded warehouse, blending and bottling facilities and purchasing two Glasgow-based businesses: a bottle manufacturer, the North British Bottle Manufacturing Co. Ltd and, in 1907, a case-making factory, the Acme Tea Chest Co. Ltd. In 1906 the company introduced the first six-bottle wooden case for the Christmas gift trade.

In 1907 the company was appointed supplier to His Imperial Majesty the Emperor of Japan and His Royal Highness the Crown Prince of Greece. *Black & White* enjoyed great export success in the years leading up to the First World War.

On 1 April 1915, in order to combat the growing competitive strength of the DCL and difficulties that had arisen as a result of the war, Buchanan amalgamated his company with John Dewar & Sons Ltd to form Scotch Whisky Brands Ltd. In 1919 the company was re-named Buchanan-Dewar Ltd.

In 1920, Buchanan, jointly with Dewar, acquired Port Ellen and Lochruan distilleries. Knighted in the same year, Buchanan became a peer two years later, taking the title of Baron Woolavington of Lavington. The acquisition of distilleries continued with the purchase in 1922, in conjunction with Dewar, of Benrinnes-Glenlivet distillery.

In 1923, along with Dewar and Walkers, they bought James Watson & Co. of Dundee and its large stocks of matured whiskies.

Buchanan and Dewar retained their separate identities until 1925, when they, along with John Walker & Sons Ltd, joined DCL in the action known as 'The Big Amalgamation'.

1923. Another appearance of the black and white terriers and a clear assurance that the company had 'the largest stocks of matured Scotch malt whiskies', enabling them 'to guarantee a continuance of the very high standard of quality of their brands'.

1924. Artist: John G. Millais, 1922.

1925. Sales in Britain of *Black & White* were nearing one million cases a year, and the brand was the second largest brand of blended Scotch whisky after *Johnnie Walker*.

1926. One of a series of silhouettes supporting, in this example, an extract from Sir Walter Scott's *The Fair Maid of Perth*.

1928. The new 'lever cap' bottle fitting is explained.

1928.

1928. Artist: Frank Reynolds. The reassurance that the brand was 'Renowned the World Over for Age and Quality' appears for the first time, and variations of the slogan were used until 1936.

1929. Artist: Arthur Wardle.

1930. Another in a fine series of drawings by Arthur Wardle of the best of dog breeds. This advertisement marks the end of an era. James Buchanan, the founder of the company, created Lord Woolavington in 1922, was a director of DCL from 1925 until his death in 1935. At some stage during 1930 the decision was taken to drop any reference in the advertisements to the family name Buchanan.

1930. The black and white dogs were used in point-of-sale advertising material but it was to be a further seven years before they became inseparable characters in the brand's magazine advertising.

1933. The first use by *Black & White* of a real photographic subject.

1935. The value of *Black & White*'s medicinal qualities is given brief promotion in a February issue of *The Illustrated Sporting and Dramatic News*.

1935. One of a splendid series of British Regiments painted by Christopher Clark.

1936. Another of Clark's British Regiments – The Gordon Highlanders – is featured on the front cover of the 7 March special point-to-point number of *The Field*.

1937. Coronation year.

1937. 'It's THE Whisky!' and it's THE arrival of the dogs!

1938. For a brief period the slogan used was 'The Scotch with Character'. This was to be used in the United States, with great success, for over twenty years.

1938. An example from the series of *Black & White* Sporting Occasions.

1939. 'It's the Scotch': a series that was used in the early part of the Second World War.

THE ILLUSTRATED LONDON NEWS CHRISTMAS NUMBER, 1948.—IV

THE ILLUSTRATED LONDON NEWS CHRISTMAS NUMBER, 1948—2

*To friends everywhere we send Greetings
and all Best Wishes for*

A MERRY CHRISTMAS AND A GOOD NEW YEAR

"BLACK & WHITE"

SCOTCH WHISKY

BY APPOINTMENT
SCOTCH WHISKY DISTILLERS
TO H.M. KING GEORGE VI.
JAMES BUCHANAN & CO. LTD

JAMES BUCHANAN & CO. LTD., SCOTCH WHISKY DISTILLERS, GLASGOW & LONDON

*To friends everywhere we send
Greetings and all Best Wishes for*

A MERRY CHRISTMAS AND A GOOD NEW YEAR

"BLACK & WHITE"

SCOTCH WHISKY

JAMES BUCHANAN & CO. LTD., SCOTCH WHISKY DISTILLERS, GLASGOW AND LONDON

(left) 1948. Mabel Gear's 'Homecoming' is one of *the* classic advertisements for any brand of Scotch whisky.

(above) 1949. Another Christmas and another classic advertisement.

(right) 1951. Artist: Mabel Gear.

*We send to all our friends at home and abroad
Greetings and Best Wishes for*

A HAPPY CHRISTMAS AND A GOOD NEW YEAR

"BLACK & WHITE"

SCOTCH WHISKY

JAMES BUCHANAN & CO., LTD., SCOTCH WHISKY DISTILLERS, GLASGOW AND LONDON *(right)* 1954. For most of the 1950s the company was attempting to regain sales lost during and after the war. The black and white dogs were to play an important role in the advertising, and by 1960 sales were at the same level as before the war, and increasing steadily.

(far right) 1957. The emphasis in advertising has moved into the area of quality and the use of the slogan 'The Secret is in the Blending'. The bottle label and advertisement both clearly incorporate, after an absence of over twenty-five years, the founding family name of 'Buchanan's'.

With a view to good entertainment

Nothing can take the place of good Scotch Whisky for entertaining and you cannot do better than serve "Black & White". The subtle qualities of this fine Scotch have won warm regard throughout the world.

'BLACK & WHITE'
SCOTCH WHISKY
The Secret is in the Blending

By Appointment to the late King George VI   Scotch Whisky Distillers James Buchanan & Co. Ltd.

Distinction through blending

From a variety of individual whiskies the blender selects those with the characteristics he desires. Carefully and skilfully he blends them in the correct proportions to achieve the quality and flavour for which "Black & White" is famous.

'BLACK & WHITE'
SCOTCH WHISKY
"BUCHANAN'S"

By Appointment Scotch Whisky Distillers to Her Majesty The Queen James Buchanan & Co. Ltd.

The Secret is in the Blending

Advertising Black & White in the United States

1942. The Scotch with Character. Before the war *Black & White* had become the largest selling brand of Scotch whisky in the United States. Sold as an eight-year-old, every effort was made to satisfy the American market, and the two terriers, Blackie and Whitey, did all they could to help the war effort. Artist: Morgan Dennis.

1944. The war effort continues but the age statement had been dropped.

1959. The long-running advertising campaign using Blackie and Whitey continued until the death of the artist, Morgan Dennis, in 1960.

Now there are two
"Black & White" Scotch Whiskies
...and one is Extra Light!

equal in quality...identical in price

In "Black & White's" Great Original Scotch, you'll find the body and bouquet of a traditional Scotch. It has the *character* that only "Black & White" knows how to give—the special character of Scotland in every drop.

"Black & White" *Extra Light* Scotch has a smooth, glowing clarity. It is not merely a *light* Scotch, but a light Scotch with the famous "Black & White" *character*. Whichever you choose—you're always right with "Black & White."

BLENDED SCOTCH WHISKY • 86.8 PROOF • THE FLEISCHMANN DISTILLING CORPORATION, N.Y.C. • SOLE DISTRIBUTORS

(above) 1965. This chapter concludes with the arrival on the American market of an Extra Light version of *Black & White* to take on the growing competition from the lighter coloured *J & B Rare* and *Cutty Sark* Scotch whiskies.

(right) 1963. A new era of leisure and glamour has dawned. There is a lady in the advertisement, whisky tumblers full to the brim, and a realisation that the Americans enjoy their *Black & White* in green bottles!

Put out the bottle that shows you know SCOTCH !
Enjoy the extra smoothness that has always given
"Black & White" a light, bright character all its own.

"BLACK & WHITE"
THE SCOTCH WITH CHARACTER

DISTILLED AND BOTTLED IN SCOTLAND • BLENDED SCOTCH WHISKY • 86.8 PROOF • THE FLEISCHMANN DISTILLING CORPORATION, N.Y.C. • SOLE DISTRIBUTORS

Chapter 6
Haig

1. "HOLLY LEAVES," CHRISTMAS NUMBER OF THE ILLUSTRATED SPORTING AND DRAMATIC NEWS, 1936.

Don't be vague –
ASK FOR
Haig

A HAPPY
CHRISTMAS

Once again the
most appropriate
accompaniment of
the wish is the truly
seasonable gift of
Haig

NO FINER WHISKY GOES INTO ANY BOTTLE

1936. 'Don't be vague – Ask for Haig'. The first colour advertisement to show the slogan that was to contribute so much to the Haig success story appeared in the Christmas number of *The Illustrated Sporting and Dramatic News*.

Haig Gold Label and *Dimple* are two world-renowned brands of blended Scotch whisky, both packaged in unique bottles and for many years advertised together using one of the most memorable advertising slogans of the last century: 'Don't be vague – Ask for *Haig*'. The two brands were brought to life by two separate branches of the Haig family, and it was not until the 1920s that for quite diverse reasons they came together under the ownership of DCL.

John Haig & Co. Ltd

The *Haig* family was of French origin, from Normandy, and settled in the Melrose area of the Scottish Borders in the middle of the twelfth century, where they built a peel tower, a modest form of castle, at a place called Bemersyde.

In 1623 Robert Haig established himself as a farmer at Throsk in the parish of St Ninian's in Stirlingshire. His early days had been spent in Holland, where he learned the art of distilling, and as was common custom with farmers, he distilled barley surplus to his needs. The first record of distilling at Throsk was believed to have been in 1627, and this fact clearly influenced Haig's advertising in the early twentieth century. Alas, Robert broke the strict rules of the Presbyterian Church for having worked his still on a Sunday, and he was summoned in January 1655 to appear before the Kirk Session where he was rebuked for having allowed his still to have been 'played' on the Sabbath.

There are records of succeeding generations of the Haig family developing strong and successful interests in distilling. It was John Haig from the sixth generation to succeed Robert Haig who established the foundations of

(far left) 1902. An early twentieth-century advertisement for John Haig's *Glenleven Old Highland Whisky*. Later advertisements claimed that the company was established in 1627 whereas this states: 'Established prior to 1680'.

Glenleven was a very important brand to John Haig for most of the first twenty years of the twentieth century. National advertising of *John Haig Liqueur Whisky* did not appear until the company had been absorbed into DCL.

(left) 1917.

the House of Haig that we see today. In 1824, at the age of twenty-two, John Haig began distilling at Cameron Bridge in Fife. Two years later Robert Stein, a cousin of the Haig's, invented the Stein 'Patent' still. The following year John Haig installed one of these stills to produce grain spirit and by the 1860s the company was producing blended whiskies. In April 1877 DCL was formed and Haig's grain distilling business was one of the six founding companies. The blending side of the business, operating as John Haig, Sons & Co., was transferred to nearby Markinch.

John Haig died in 1878. In 1882 the company merged with David Smith & Co. of Leith and use was made of Smith's bonded warehouse until one was built at Markinch in 1892.

On 4 April 1894, John Haig & Co. was registered as a limited company and Hugh Veitch Haig, John Haig's eldest son, became the company's first chairman. Also appointed to the company's board of directors was Captain Douglas Haig, the youngest of John Haig's family of eleven children. His great military career in the Sudan, South Africa and India and throughout the First World War was honoured shortly after the war when he was created Earl Haig and given the Order of Merit. He died in 1928 and, at his own request, was buried in Dryburgh Abbey beside the grave of Sir Walter Scott.

1919. The First World War was a very difficult period for all distillers and the restrictions imposed by the government on availability of stocks continued after 1918. That message is contained in this January 1919 advertisement in *The Sphere* but not until a withering attack had been made on the defeated 'Hun-beast'. The German navy, having 'tamely handed over his fleet without clearing the decks for one last effort', surprised all when they scuttled their fleet in the Scapa Flow on 21 June 1919.

(above) 1923. *Punch*: 22 August 1923. Shortly after DCL and the 'Big Three' had bought the whisky stocks and brands of Haig & Haig from the liquidated company Robertson & Baxter, DCL set about jointly marketing *John Haig Liqueur Whisky* and *Dimple Scots* – the new brand name for *Haig & Haig Five Stars Scots Whisky*. This is probably the first advertisement showing the two brands together and under a slogan adopted the year before: 'D'ye Ken John Haig'.

(above right) 1922. Haig had faith that 'D'ye Ken John Haig' was a strong enough advertising slogan without any illustration of the whisky bottle to continue the development of awareness of the company's brands. Christopher Clark illustrated three series of advertisements with informative text on a wide range of subjects. There were twenty-four advertisements in the Clubland series detailing the history and activities of *inter alia* the obscure Rota, Cocoa, Green Ribbon and Robin Hood clubs.

(above far right) 1923. 'A Chaucerian Club.'

To ensure the supply of good Highland malt whisky, the company bought Glen Cawdor distillery in Nairn in 1903 and by that date large offices had been opened in London and Manchester. John Haig and Co. Ltd merged with DCL in 1919 and, following the amalgamation of the 'Big Three' and DCL in 1925, Haig & Haig Ltd was made a subsidiary of John Haig & Co. Ltd.

Haig & Haig Ltd

The firm of Haig & Haig Ltd was established in 1888 by John Alicius Haig, the brother of John Haig & Co.'s director, Hugh Veitch Haig, to market whisky in the United States. George Ogilvy Haig introduced the unique 'pinched decanter' bottle shape in 1893 and the brand was known for the first thirty years of its life as *Haig & Haig Five Stars Scots Whisky*. During the First World War the use of the 'pinched decanter' bottle was temporarily discontinued and replaced by a standard bottle described in advertisements as the 'substituted war bottle'. Before 1920, when Prohibition prevented the importation of

Scotch whisky into the United States, *Haig & Haig Five Star* (sic) *Scots Whisky* had become a leading brand.

Following the liquidation in 1907 of Haig & Haig Ltd, Robertson and Baxter took control of the company. In 1922 members of the Robertson family not actively involved in the business decided to sell out and realise their investment. This involved Robertson and Baxter going into voluntary liquidation in 1922. DCL and the 'Big Three' (Buchanan-Dewar and Walkers) paid over £1 million for the company, its stock of 2 million gallons of whisky and its brands including *Haig & Haig Five Stars Scots Whisky*. DCL had wanted to be part of this deal in order that it could suppress the *Haig & Haig* brand because its presence conflicted with the development of *John Haig's Liqueur Whisky* that had been acquired in 1919 when they took over John Haig & Co. Ltd. For the purposes of bootlegging

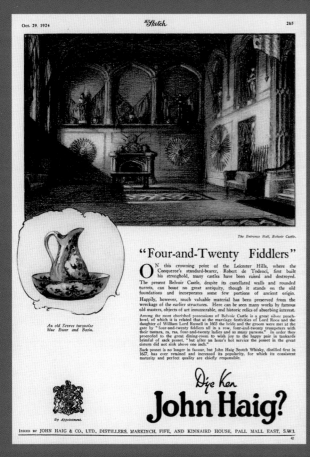

1924. The Famous Rooms series contained thirty-six subjects, including this carefully crafted drawing of the Entrance Hall at Belvoir Castle in Leicestershire.

1924. *The Times of India Annual* contained a full-page advertisement with the same message as in Britain: 'D'ye Ken John Haig – The Clubman's whisky since 1627'. India was a very important and well-developed export market for many brands of Scotch whisky.

1925. A full page in *Punch* is dominated by a heavily branded presence of the two brands. The *John Haig* label bears for the first time the all important description: '*GOLD LABEL*'.

1923. The John Haig Famous Hostelry series: The George, Huntingdon

1925. With both companies fully owned by DCL, the *Gold Label's* re-designed label states: 'John Haig & Co. Ltd *incorporating* Haig & Haig Ltd'. Later advertisements simplify this to 'John Haig & Co. Ltd *owning* Haig & Haig Ltd'.

1925. Artist: unsigned, but in the style of the Beggarstaff Brothers.

1925. A new slogan: 'The Father of all Scotch whiskies'. Artist: Nunney.

1926. The Royal and Ancient Golf Club, St Andrews. The clubhouse overlooking the first tee of the famous Old Course was built in 1854, exactly 100 years after The Society of St Andrews Golfers was founded. In 1834 the Society changed its name to the Royal and Ancient Golf Club of St Andrews. Artist: Christopher Clark.

1927. Haig's Tercentenary year was an excellent opportunity to link highway robbers in 1627 with income tax in 1927! Artist: Christopher Clark.

1927. An Australian advertisement for *John Haig Gold Label*. Australia
was another very important and well-established market for Haig.

(above) 1927. For a brief period between December 1927 and April 1928, Haig whiskies were marketed as 'The Empire Whisky' and, with a General Election looming, the company's advertising attacked the grossly unfair 'war' tax on Scotch whisky.

(above right) 1928.

(far right) 1928. This group of advertisements marked the end of the era of *John Haig*: the whiskies were sold simply as *Haig* whisky.

in the United States, and rather than develop a new brand, the 'Big Three' wanted to revive *Haig & Haig* and capitalise on the value of the brand, its heavy advertising in the past and its leading brand position in the United States. This argument won the day and following the merger of the 'Big Three' with DCL in 1925, Haig & Haig Ltd was made a subsidiary of John Haig.

The first indication of the brand name *Dimple Scots* appearing on a label of the pinched decanter bottle was in 1923. This bottle was advertised alongside *John Haig's Liqueur Whisky*. All references in any advertising in the home market of *Haig & Haig Five Stars Scots Whisky* were removed. William Williamson of Haig & Haig Ltd joined John Gillon & Co. Ltd of Leith and London, blenders of *King William IV VOP (Very Old Particular) Six Stars Scots Whisky*. Their advertising in 1923 referred to his role as chairman and managing director of the company and that *King William IV* was a suitable alternative to *Haig & Haig*. This competitive situation was short-lived: Gillons was acquired by DCL in 1925.

After the repeal of Prohibition in the United States the 'pinched decanter' bottle was sold as *Haig & Haig* and sold alongside *Haig and Haig Five Star Scots Whisky*. In the early 1950s *Haig & Haig* began to be marketed as *Haig & Haig*

Pinch, and in 1958 the uniquely shaped bottle was patented. The gilded wire mesh net around the bottle, which was specially made in France, was introduced to prevent the cork stopper from becoming loose whilst being shipped to export markets. The introduction of a new closure in 1973 coincided with the removal of the gilded net.

Dimple was one of a number of brands removed by DCL from the British market between 1977 and 1983 to counter difficulties of trading at different prices in the European market. In 1988 the brand experienced a makeover and, as well as being made available at twelve or fifteen years old, the wire net was restored.

1931. 'Why be vague? Ask for Haig'. It took a little while during the 1930s for the great one-liner to be created. It was almost there in January 1931. The supporting line, 'No finer whisky goes into any bottle', is first seen here and in many advertisements until its last use in 1956.

1931. The cunning use of the letters and apostrophe in *Haig's Whisky* will lead to the slogan that was to last for many years.

1932. 'Say 'Haig' – why be vague?'... nearly there. This advertisement was Haig's first use of real photographic subjects and their first to associate the drinking of whisky with the environment of sport and leisure activities.

1932. The first 'Don't be vague – ask for Haig' appeared in a full-page advertisement in the 10 December issue of *The Illustrated London News*.

1933. But it is not yet set in stone! 'Don't be vague *order* Haig'.

1936. At last there is no vagueness in the campaign.

1937. Classless Haig.

1949. Artist: Unsigned, this is the work of Kapra.

NO FINER WHISKY GOES INTO ANY BOTTLE

Good Scotch Whisky is the friendliest of all spirits, mellow, kindly stimulating, a smoothly satisfying drink for all occasions. Its superlative merit is due to the unique virtues inherent in its production which cannot be imitated, and the scrupulous care taken in its blending and maturing by the great distillers of Scotland. So stick to Scotch— and give it a name . . .

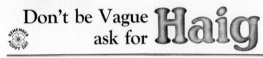

Don't be Vague ask for Haig

1952. A further change to the label: it is now *Haig's Gold Label*.

1950. Following agreement within the Scotch whisky industry to avoid confusion over the use of the description 'Liqueur', the word has been removed from the label.

Christmas 1952.

1956.

1967. From *John Haig & Co. Ltd Gold Label Liqueur Blended Whisky* in 1925, the brand is now in its simplest form: *HAIG Gold Label Blended Scotch Whisky*.

1975. Three basic ingredients of classical whisky advertising of the period: a background of golf, a bottle of *Haig* and whisky tumblers with a good measure of plain, straightforward *Haig*.

Advertising Haig in the United States

1943. The sales strength of Haig & Haig brands that had existed in the United States before Prohibition was developed further after Repeal in 1933. A 1943 advertisement shows the eight-years-old *Five Star* alongside the twelve-years-old *Haig & Haig* in the 'Pinch Bottle'.

1976. By the mid-1970s there was considerable competitive pressure on *Haig* in the buoyant Scotch whisky market in the UK, both from within DCL with its *Johnnie Walker, White Horse* and *Black & White*, and elsewhere from Bell's, Teacher's and The Famous Grouse. *Haig*'s supremacy at the time of the outbreak of the Second World War had been toppled, but all was not lost. As with many other brands of blended whisky there had been since the 1920s an increasingly close association with the main sporting interests of cricket and golf, and this was frequently to be seen in advertising themes. *Haig* went a stage further and incorporated into its advertising and promotional strategy the sponsorship of village cricket, and launched in 1972 the Haig Village Cricket Championship. By its fifth year there were 834 participating teams trying to secure a place in the final at Lord's. In 1975 *Haig* extended its cricket sponsorship to club level, involving 256 clubs competing for a place in the final at Lord's and the award of the John Haig Trophy.

1947. Haig & Haig's decanter is one of the greatest bottle designs of all time and has enjoyed huge sales success. The bottle shape was 'trademarked' in the UK in 1923 and patented in the United States in 1958. Artist: Kapra.

1950.

1948.

In unvarying high quality and mellow flavor Haig & Haig Scotch Whisky reflects the world-wide reputation of Scotland's oldest distillers. Today the demand for this famous Scotch Whisky is greater than ever before.

Don't be Vague... say **Haig & Haig**

BLENDED SCOTS WHISKY, 86.8 PROOF • RENFIELD IMPORTERS LTD., NEW YORK

1955. *Pinch* was incorporated into the brand name in the early 1950s.

Quality runs in the family...

1960 marks the end of an era and the beginning of another when a bold move was made to bring the *Five Star* up-to-date by changing the design and colour of the bottle.

Chapter 7
White Horse

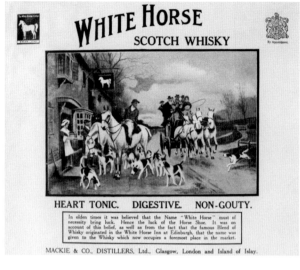

1903. A first tentative step into advertising two years after the company's decision to sell *Mackie's White Horse Cellar Scotch Whisky* in the UK. The use of NB in Scottish addresses, the abbreviation for North Britain, was quite the norm in the late nineteenth and early twentieth century. This advertisement appeared in *TP's Weekly*, a newspaper founded in 1902 by an Irishman, Thomas Power O'Connor, who had worked in London for *The Daily Telegraph*, and holding radical political opinions he stood for Parliament in the 1880 General Election. He successfully became Irish Nationalist Member of Parliament for Galway. *TP's Weekly* was O'Connor's third publication following *The Star*, a radical newspaper founded in 1887, and *The Sun* in 1893.

(above right) 1910. Substantial growth in sales and a Royal warrant gave Mackie & Co. the stimulus to embark on some serious advertising. It is a delight to read of the brand's special qualities: Heart tonic, Digestive and Non-gouty!

The history of the firm that eventually became White Horse Distillers Ltd can be traced back to 1801, when William Graham established himself in business in Glasgow. Thirty years later Alexander Graham entered the business and in 1845 James Logan Mackie became a partner. At some point shortly after that date the firm became known as J. Logan Mackie & Co. (Distillers) and in 1867 it bought the Islay distillery, Lagavulin. Mackie's nephew, Peter Jeffrey Mackie, became a partner in 1878.

In 1890 the name of the company was changed to Mackie & Co. Distillers Ltd and, in addition to distilling and blending *Mackie's White Horse Cellar Scotch Whisky*, they handled brandies and clarets and acted as sales agents for Laphroaig whisky. The name *White Horse* was probably chosen because an old coaching inn of that name in Edinburgh's Canongate was situated close to the home that had been in the hands of generations of the Mackie family since 1650. It is also highly likely that Peter Mackie, who passionately believed that whisky should be sold with maturity, quality and age, found particular appeal in a White Horse which has always been symbolical of purity and high ideal.

'Restless Peter' Mackie, described by Sir Robert Bruce Lockhart in his book *Scotch* as 'one-third genius, one-third megalomaniac, one-third eccentric', was a remarkable man who, with boundless energy and integrity, developed the foundations of White Horse Distillers. In 1891, in partnership with Alexander Edward, Mackie built Craigellachie distillery on Speyside, and in 1916 he took full control of it. One point on which Mackie was most insistent was that good whisky was sold only when it had been matured for at least three years. This indeed became a legal requirement during the First World War.

White Horse was registered as a brand in 1891 and great efforts were made to develop the export trade of the firm. It was not until 1901 that *White Horse* was made available on the home market. In 1905 Mackie revealed to his shareholders that the launch had been disappointing:

> We had not calculated the immense sum required for advertising, owing to the ignorance of a large section of the English public in regard to quality. The result was that we dropped nearly £30,000 in that venture. Luckily we had good business elsewhere, otherwise it would have been a serious affair.

White Horse won many awards for its excellence at overseas exhibitions, and in 1908 was awarded the Grand Prix at the Franco-British Exhibition in London. In the same year HM King Edward VII awarded the Royal Warrant to the

1921. Mackie's can trace its corporate origin to 1801 and therefore the reference to *White Horse* having been established in 1742 needs some further examination. The clue lies in the area of the parish of Kildalton on Islay's south coast, where Lagavulin distillery was established in an area believed to be the oldest whisky-distilling district on the island. In Alfred Barnard's book of 1887, based on his visit to every distillery in the United Kingdom (which then included all of Ireland), he noted that he had been informed that:

> ... around 1742 there were ten small and separate smuggling bothys [sic] for the manufacture of 'moonlight', which when working presented anything but a true picture of 'still life', and were all subsequently absorbed into one establishment, the whole work not making more than a few thousand gallons per annum'.

That one establishment was Lagavulin distillery and therefore *White Horse*'s direct link with the distillery gives it the unquestionable right to say: 'Established 1742'. By 1921 Mackie's owned four distilleries. Malt Mill was built alongside Lagavulin by Mackie in 1908 after he had lost the agency for Laphroaig's whisky the year before. With its own maltings, two wash backs and two pear-shaped stills modelled on the design of Laphroaig, Malt Mill produced a truly traditional Islay malt aimed at the same market as Laphroaig's. The distillery survived long after Mackie's death in 1924, and it was eventually closed in 1960 and dismantled two years later to make way for the expansion of Lagavulin distillery. Craigellachie came under Mackie's full control in 1916. Through the purchase of Greenlees & Colvill Ltd in 1920, Mackie acquired Hazelburn, the largest distillery in Campbeltown. Production there ceased in 1925.

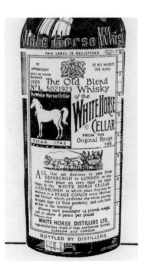

1925. The *White Horse* bottle label.

1925. A white horse has long been a symbol of purity and high ideal, of power and righteousness and an omen of victory. The Saxon Generals, Hengist and Horsa, were mounted on white horses and Napoleon always rode one. White horses are embodied in the heraldic designs of family crests and in the arms of several guilds including farriers, innholders and saddlers.

The Cherhill white horse is an example from a series of advertisements depicting white horses in the English countryside. The origins of white horses cut out of the chalk hills are uncertain, although there is a strong belief that they may have derived from horse worship. The oldest of England's twenty-one white horses still visible to the naked eye was created during the Bronze Age at Uffington in Oxfordshire. Of the thirteen known sites in Wiltshire, eight are still visible. The illustrated Cherhill horse, also known as the Oldbury white horse, is situated about four miles east of Calne on the Cherhill Downs, and dates back to 1780. The site is just below Oldbury Castle, an old hill fort, and close to the obelisk known as the Lansdowne Monument. The horse was created by first cutting the shape in the grassy topsoil and then removing the grass and soil to expose the chalk beneath. The horse was the work of Dr Christopher Allsop, the 'Mad Doctor' who was Guild Steward of the Borough of Calne. It is rumoured that he shouted his instructions for the cutting of the horse through a speaking trumpet from a position in Cherhill village, 1.5 miles away. Dr Allsop's design for the trotting horse may have been influenced by the work of his artist friend George Stubbs, famous for his paintings of horses and other animals.

This advertisement was to be one of the last before White Horse Distillers Ltd lost its independence when taken over by DCL in 1927.

The Sketch

THE OLDEST HORSE IN THE WORLD.
Incomparable whisky—Incomparable bottle. Opened in
an instant—no corkscrew required

1928. 'Opened in an instant… no corkscrew required'. In 1926 the company introduced the first screw-cap closure in the industry and this produced a remarkable doubling of sales in six months. This was *White Horse*'s first colour advertisement.

company as distillers of blended whiskies.

After the restrictions on distilling imposed by the government during the First World War, the company was short of capital to buy stocks to satisfy increasing overseas sales. In 1923 Mackie discussed a possible merger with Buchanan-Dewar, but they wanted *White Horse* to be taken off the market. There was no way that he could agree to that demand and, although further discussions were held, no financial basis for a merger could be arranged.

In 1924, shortly after Mackie & Co., Distillers, Ltd was reconstituted as White Horse Distillers, Mackie died at the age of sixty-nine. In June 1927 the company became the last of the 'Big Five', following Haig, Dewar, Buchanan and Walkers, to be taken over by DCL.

Shortly after Mackie's death the various diverse commercial activities that he had developed after the war were given up. The company had been producing Highland Tweeds; distilling and selling Holloway's London Gin; producing cattle cake; selling Carragheen Moss; manufacturing concrete slabs and partitions, and a patent flour sold as BBM: Brain, Bone and Muscle!

In an article on the historical development of *White Horse* whisky in the April 1933 issue of the DCL house magazine, *DCL Gazette*, there was this delightful concluding paragraph:

> What the Gods may have in store for *White Horse* in years to come we know not, but the enthusiasm and *esprit de corps* of Directors and staff at home and abroad are such that we can afford to close this little history on an optimistic note. The lusty infant of but a few years ago has grown into a strong, healthy child, worthy of the full rights of membership of the DCL Group.

1929. The copy describes the marrying process in the latter stages of maturing *White Horse*. This blending and re-blending would probably have set *White Horse* apart from other blended whiskies, and was intended to give assurance of the brand's special quality.

1931. Christmas joy in the form of the '*White Horse* Three Valve' three-bottle gift box and an alternative two-bottle 'Lucky Horseshoe' gift pack.

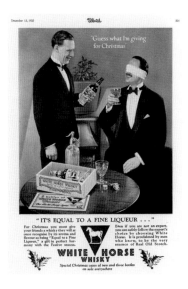

1933. An example from the slightly unusual campaign featuring blindfolds and the copy line 'Equal to a fine liqueur', in use until 1939.

1943. 'Ah! This is good whisky'. It is fair to say that in the copy there is a hint that you may be, after four years in a war, 'jaded in body and mind'!

1950. The highwayman is in need of a White Horse! *White Horse*'s rare and special qualities of excellence are spelled out: fragrance, softness, a glorious afterglow. The bottom line of the advertisement indicates the maximum retail prices as fixed by the Scotch Whisky Association following 'Austerity' Cripps' 1948 Budget. The standard bottle was 33*s* 4*d* (£1.66).

1952. The cocktail bar is where aspiring whisky drinkers will find the 'noble' *White Horse*.

April 23, 1955 — THE ILLUSTRATED LONDON NEWS — 721

Not born yesterday

How pleasant sometimes to stand aside.
To slip into an older, gentler world.
To think that even now some things take
years, not minutes, to produce. To remember that no-one and
nothing can hurry the slow, subtle ageing of White
Horse Whisky, transmuting its ardour to a soft and
golden glow. Even in these feverish days there are
times when Time itself has to stand almost still.

WHITE HORSE
Scotch Whisky

1955. There are some gems contained in the copy of old advertisements. Time has a very special effect on the maturation of *White Horse*: 'no-one and nothing can hurry the slow, subtle ageing of White Horse Whisky, transmuting its ardour to a soft and golden glow.'

1957.

"I think I'd like a little whisky.
I happen to know they've some White Horse."

1956. A rare example of the exclusion of both the *White Horse* bottle and logo from the brand's advertising.

Winter Wisdom

WHEN chills are in the air the way to
keep the cold out is to be warm
within. Towards bed-time take a
little White Horse with hot
lemon and sugar or in hot milk.
Let sound sleep and the soothing
glow of this fine Scotch whisky
drive off the questing germs
of colds and influenza. There is
no more pleasant precaution.

1957.

576 — THE ILLUSTRATED LONDON NEWS — OCTOBER 12, 1957

WHITE HORSE

To pour out White Horse Scotch Whisky
for friends who really understand whisky
is a particular pleasure. Warmth, bouquet
and flavour, name and fame all combine
in the grand total of their enjoyment.

To offer White Horse to your friends
defines the standards of your hospitality.
With every drop they taste a welcome far
warmer than mere words.

Scotch Whisky

COUNTRY LIFE—SEPTEMBER 27, 1962

1962. An example from the series: 'There's no mistaking White Horse'.

1969. Three examples from the very powerful, surreal campaign that had
begun in 1967: 'You can take a White Horse anywhere'.

1970.

You can take a White Horse anywhere.

FINE OLD SCOTCH WHISKY.

1973.

Did It Taste Any Better When It Was 3/6 A Bottle?

3/6 was a lot of money in those days. Fine old whisky like White Horse was never cheap.

But people who bought it judged their money well spent, and came back for more.

They came back when White Horse went to 4/0 just before World War I. And 12/6 afterwards.

And 14/3 in 1939. And £1.15s in 1952. And £2.55p in 1971.

And they came back for a good reason. Whatever else was changing in the world, White Horse was staying the same. The same quality. The same character. The same fine old Scotch whisky.

Today, we know more and more of you are worried that more and more things aren't what they used to be.

Take heart. That old White Horse whisky isn't going to change at any price.

It's Still The Same Old Scotch.

1975. The simple answer of course has to be 'No!' Against a background of price changes between 1914 and the early 1970s, *White Horse* gives the simple assurance that the brand has not changed: 'same quality, same character'. There has, however, been a significant change to the amount of detail on the label.

Chapter 8

VAT 69

1924. For thirty years, 'Quality Tells', two simple and memorable words, appeared on almost all advertisements for *VAT 69*. The slogan was devised by the founder's son, William Mark Sanderson, and is reproduced in advertisements as a facsimile of his handwriting.

W illiam Sanderson was born in Leith in 1839 and at the age of twenty-four he established himself in Charlotte Lane, Leith, as a wine merchant and manufacturer of cordials and liqueurs. Within his wide range of products, his Rich Green Ginger Wine, Raspberry Cordial and Rhubarb Wine became most popular. William also made up a number of special blends of whisky for an increasing number of customers in Britain and in Europe. In 1876 William extended his premises and took out a licence to become a spirit dealer and wholesaler. His son,

William Mark, joined the business in 1880. Although a good deal of whisky was sold in casks, both to households and public houses, William Mark persuaded his father to seek out a blended whisky to sell in a bottle. William made up nearly 100 different blends and asked a group of friends and skilled blenders to choose from this large selection the blend of their choice. There was a remarkable consensus that the best was in vat number 69, and therefore he followed the logic of simplicity, named the blend *VAT 69*, selected a bottle that could be made locally in Leith and the

1926. Not a subject that would be used today!

1928. *VAT 69*'s first in colour advertisement was placed in *The Illustrated London News*.

1929. Many of the early *VAT 69* advertisements were heavily branded and the bottle was always strongly featured.

(right) 1932.

(far right) 1933. Sanderson's amalgamated with Booth's Distilleries in 1933. Little is known about T. Grainger Jeffrey, the artist of this fine painting of the winning horse.

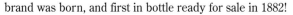

brand was born, and first in bottle ready for sale in 1882!

Following the setting up of DCL in 1877, and in fear of that company having a monopoly of supply of grain whisky, William Sanderson, along with John Crabbie and Andrew Usher and other blenders and whisky merchants, decided to build their own patent still distillery in Edinburgh. Work on building the North British distillery was started in 1885 and two years later it was in production, with Sanderson as its first managing director.

To ensure an adequate supply of quality malts for his blend, Sanderson went into partnership with John Begg at Royal Lochnagar distillery, and in 1886 he became a partner with Robert Harvey Thomson at Glengarioch distillery. Following the death of Thomson in 1897, Sanderson took full control of Glengarioch. By the turn of the century the

company had developed a flourishing export business and was particularly successful in Australia, South Africa, Canada and Europe. Sanderson died in 1908 and was succeeded by his son. In 1929, following the death of William Mark, a third generation of Sanderson, William's son Kenneth, took control of the company. After a number of difficult years of trading, the company amalgamated in 1935 with gin-producers Booth's Distilleries Ltd, owners of Stromness, Royal Brackla and Millburn malt distilleries, and two years later became part of DCL.

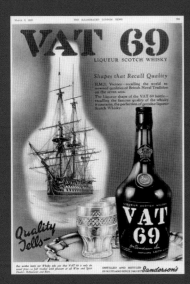

1935. Sanderson's pride in the unique shape of the bottle inspired the series: 'Shapes that Recall Quality'.

1936. The company was granted the Royal Warrant by the Prince of Wales in 1936 and the 'By Appointment' is well to the fore in the advertisement.

1937. The Coronation of King George VI and Queen Elizabeth is the subject of a special full-page advertisement in *The Illustrated London News* Coronation Record Number. This was one occasion when the slogan 'Quality Tells' was deemed to have been inappropriate.

(right) 1950. After the war, advertising resumed with 'The Spirit of Scotland' series with the additional qualification: 'The Distinctive Whisky in a Distinctive Bottle'. The first subject was Robert Burns and his cottage in Ayr.

(far right) 1951. The clubhouse of the Royal and Ancient Golf Club in St Andrews is another example in the 'Spirit of Scotland' series. The detail of the wax seal on the shoulder of the bottle can be clearly seen with the Sanderson family crest of a Talbot Hound, a large hunting dog that fell out of favour and was no longer bred after the early 1900s. The family motto is just visible: 'Sans Dieu Rien'.

(above) 1956. The time has arrived for a period of humour and in this case the last appearance in an advertisement of 'Quality Tells'.

(right) 1959. The cartoon illustrations in this group of advertisements have all the hallmarks of the work of Sir Osbert Lancaster.

(far right) 1961.

SUPPLEMENT TO THE ILLUSTRATED LONDON NEWS

*Everyone has a "double"—
when it's Vat 69!*

1960.

1963.

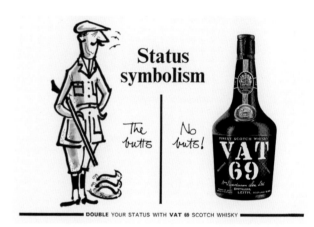

Chapter 9
Other Blended Whiskies

Baird-Taylor Bros., Ltd

Little is known of this company, other than it was established in Glasgow in 1838, developing a small whisky wholesaling business, and was bought by DCL in 1935 for £225,000. *Red Tape* whisky was advertised enthusiastically across the UK in the 1920s.

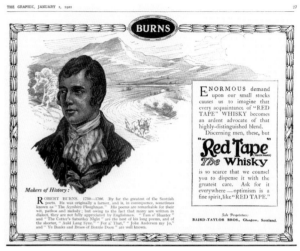

(*left*) 1920. Baird-Taylor's blended whisky was *Red Tape*, and the examples of advertising are from a six-year period between 1920 and 1925. In the period after the First World War the company was in a similar position to its competitors, short of maturing whisky stocks. The advertising mentions this and for good measure, lest there were any thoughts of temperance, '*Red Tape* is in demand for beverage and medicinal use everywhere'.

(*above*) 1921. The 'Makers of History' series. The company appears to revel in advertising its small and scarce stocks.

(*below and right*) 1922. Yachting, otter hunting, curling and fox hunting are used as advertising vehicles to convey messages of luxurious whisky to be asked for by name, and a pledge from the Sole Proprietors that it is: 'a whisky of quality, very old, pure and aristocratic'.

The huge growth of DCL occurring in the twenty or so years between 1916 and 1937 could perhaps be called the Great Period of Acquisition. This was when the company bought or amalgamated with many large and small companies, acquiring their brands, their malt and grain distilleries and stocks of maturing whisky, and established sales of whisky in the home and overseas markets. Above all else, DCL was the biggest company in the Scotch whisky industry and it found itself having to take on an unusual and developing responsibility to attempt to keep the whisky industry on an even keel in decades of troubled trading times. Once acquired by DCL, brands were either actively developed with advertising and other sales and marketing support in Britain and in selected markets overseas, or killed off at the earliest opportunity.

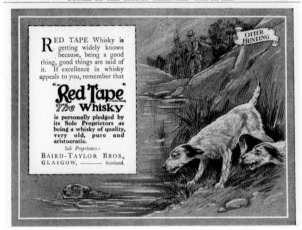

(left) All 1922.

1923. An example of the 'By-gone London' series where time is an enigma sweeping away picturesque London while *Red Tape* mellows into the most seductive whisky that ever gladdened man. That was the way to write good copy!

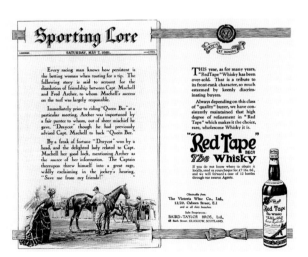

1925. We learn a little of Fred Archer being importuned by a fair punter and that *Red Tape* has been over-sold. All is not lost. *Red Tape* is available at all branches of the Victoria Wine Co. and through the company's agent: a cheque for £7 16s (£7.80p) will secure the delivery of twelve bottles.

John Begg Ltd

A former illicit distiller, James Robertson of Crathie built the first licensed Lochnagar distillery in 1826 on the north side of the river Dee. In 1841 rival unlicensed distillers burned it down and a new distillery was built four years later, by John Begg, on a site on the south side of the Dee a short distance from Balmoral Castle. Begg called his distillery New Lochnagar. In 1848, shortly after Queen Victoria had taken up residence at Balmoral, she paid a visit to the distillery, accompanied by her consort, Prince Albert. The visit was a tremendous success for John Begg, for a few days later, he was delighted to receive the news that he had been awarded the grant of a Royal Warrant of Appointment as a supplier to the Queen, and the distillery was immediately re-named Royal Lochnagar. By the time of Begg's death in 1880, he had developed a large trade in blended whisky at home and abroad. The distillery remained in the ownership of the Begg family until 1916, when DCL, seeking to enlarge its export trade in blended whisky, acquired all the shares owned by the Begg family.

1924. 29 May: 'Oak Apple (or Royal Oak) Day'. Cromwell had condemned King Charles I to death in 1649, the same year that Britain had been declared a republic. The King's son Charles escaped from the Roundheads at the Battle of Worcester on 6 September 1651, and was saved from capture by his pursuers by hiding in an oak tree in the grounds of Boscobel Hall in Staffordshire. After nine years wandering through Europe, Charles issued a Declaration that promised a general amnesty and freedom of conscience. Parliament accepted and he was proclaimed king and crowned King Charles II of Great Britain and Ireland on 29 May 1660.

1940. In *A Book of Words: Whisky*, Gavin Smith describes 'peg' as a slang term for a drink of spirits. In the seventeenth century, silver 'peg' tankards had small silver pegs on the inside to mark the diminishing contents. The tankards would usually hold two quarts and would be pegged at half-pint intervals. By today's standards that was a very large and generous measure, and presumably the recommended standard measure of *John Begg*!

1924. *John Begg*'s 'Old Time Customs' series. St James's Day falls on 25 July and St James is the patron saint of oyster fisheries.

1913. This drawing by John Hassall was used again as a full-page advertisement in an August 1923 edition of *The Illustrated London News* describing *B.L. Gold Label* as: 'A whisky of fine character for the occasions of old-fashioned friendly hospitality'. There is little evidence to be seen of any hospitality here!

The distilleries referred to at Glasgow, Islay and Campbeltown are Camlachie, Caol Ila and Benmore respectively.

Bulloch Lade & Co. Ltd

Bulloch Lade & Co. dates back to the merger in 1855 of Bulloch & Co. and D. Lade & Co., owners of the Camlachie distillery that in 1870 was re-named Loch Katrine. The company bought Caol Ila distillery on Islay in 1863, and five years later built Benmore distillery in Campbeltown.

Like many other companies, Bulloch Lade struggled through the first two decades of the twentieth century and went into liquidation in 1920. Its business, together with Caol Ila and Loch Katrine distilleries, was taken over by a consortium of whisky firms led by DCL. Trading as the Caol Ila Distillery Co. Ltd, the business was managed by the Glasgow distilling and blending company, Robertson & Baxter Ltd. Loch Katrine distillery was closed in 1920, and Caol Ila was bought by DCL in 1927. Benmore distillery had also been sold in 1920 in a separate deal, to the Glasgow-based firm of Benmore Distilleries Ltd, owners of Lochindaal, Lochhead and Dallas Dhu distilleries, and this company was acquired by DCL in 1929.

COMALA.

Her red cheek rests upon her arm, the mountain wind is in her hair. She turns her blue eyes toward the fields of his promise. Where art thou, O Fingal? The night is gathering around!

(above) 1923. An unusual and striking subject for a full-page advertisement in *The London Illustrated News.*

(above right) 1923. Comala, the daughter of Sarno, King of the Orkneys, is another character depicted in this series based on the poems of Ossian.

(right) 1926. The retail price has been reduced to 12s 6d (62.5p) per bottle, the maximum price recommended to the whisky trade by the Scotch Whisky Association.

The *original*, exclusive, old fashioned "B.L." blended by Bulloch, Lade and possessing a peculiarly characteristic Highland and Hebridean bouquet. A Whisky of pre-war quality and superior strength (25 u.p.)—well favoured by those who know, who really know, whisky: costing 15/- per bottle, yet not costly, for each bottle yields more glasses—with richer contentment in every glass.

BULLOCH, LADE & CO. LTD.
GLASGOW.   LONDON.

1924. Fine words for an exclusive whisky retailing at 15s (75p) a bottle.

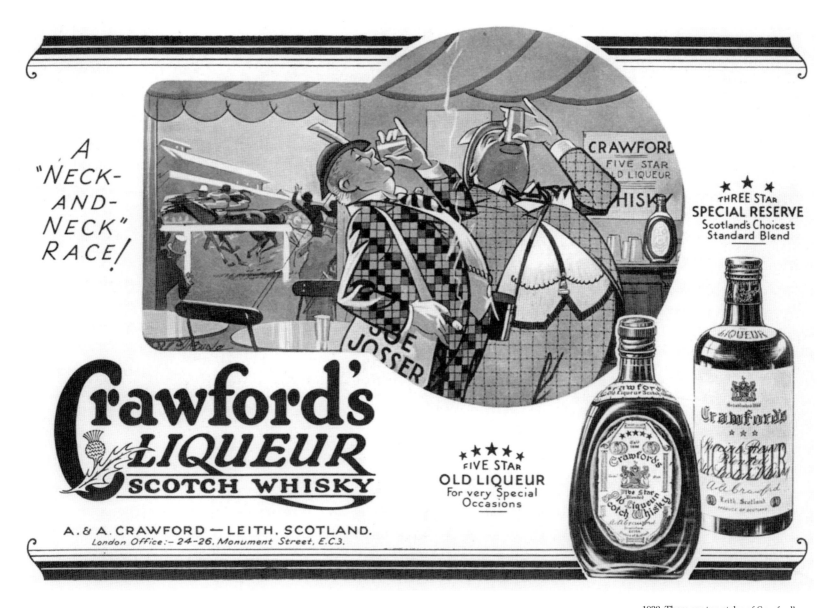

1932. There are two styles of Crawford's Liqueur Scotch Whisky – *Five Star Old Liqueur* and *Three Star Special Reserve*.

A & A Crawford Ltd

Two brothers, Archibald and Aikman Crawford, established this business of whisky blenders and merchants in 1860 in Leith. By 1885 the brothers had died and David Ireland became senior partner and was entrusted with training Harry and Archie, the sons of the original partners. In the years following the First World War, the company had considerable success with its *Three Star Special Reserve* blended whisky in the home and export markets. The business was formed into a limited company in 1942 and was bought by DCL in 1944.

(above right) 1934. The Three Stars have been removed.

(right) 1935.

(far right) 1963. The Three Stars have returned.

Peter Dawson Ltd

The company was established in Glasgow in 1882, and retained its status as a family concern until it was incorporated into DCL in 1925. The founder, Peter Dawson, built Towiemore distillery near Dufftown in 1896 and prudently sold it two years later, just before the Pattison crash. Two years before being taken over by DCL the company had, in conjunction with Macdonald, Greenlees & Williams Ltd and James Watson & Co. Ltd. of Dundee, bought Balmenach distillery near Grantown-on-Spey.

1922. *Peter Dawson Scotch Whisky* is: 'a brand of historic lineage'.

January 1924. Something extraordinary has happened to *P.D.* Its bottle has suddenly developed a very special unique selling point, a rash of bumps and depressions, or in plain marketing terms – 'brambles' and 'dimples'. The advertisement reminds you when next at your local dealer *P.D.*, that genuinely old, time-matured, wood-matured Whisky (of historic lineage), is 'brambling with pride' and 'dimpling with pleasure'. For added endorsement, *Peter Dawson 'Special' Scotch Whisky* is 'By Appointment to the King of Spain' and *P.D.* is the Whisky for Whisky and Soda.

W & A Gilbey Ltd

On their return from the Crimean War in 1857, two brothers, Walter and Alfred Gilbey, set up a wine business in London's Oxford Street. The business developed well, importing wines, sherry and port, and within two years they had opened branches in Dublin and Edinburgh. In 1887, the year of Queen Victoria's Golden Jubilee, Gilbey's became the first non-Scottish firm to buy a malt whisky distillery: Glen Spey in Rothes. Eight years later they purchased Strathmill distillery in Keith, and Knockando became their third Speyside distillery in 1904. During the 1890s Gilbey's introduced *Spey-Royal* whisky, sold for the first ten years as a rather 'heavy' vatted malt. The company was adamant that genuine whisky could not be produced, except from malted barley, and that customers asking for whisky were entitled to receive spirit distilled from that and no other grain. In W & A Gilbey's 1896 trade price list, *Spey-Royal* was described as the 'Choicest and oldest procurable. Distilled from selected Malted Barley grown in the Highlands.'

Seeing, however, the rapid development in the market for blended whiskies in England and in many overseas markets, Gilbey's had by 1905 changed the blend of *Spey-Royal*, introducing grain whisky to produce a balanced and lighter whisky.

With the purchase in 1875 of the Bordeaux property of Chateau Loudenne, Gilbey's became the first British firm to have bought a French vineyard with its own chateau. Four years later, the company began distilling London dry gin at Camden Town, and expansion of their interests continued in the early twentieth century with the purchase in 1910 of the Port House, Croft & Co., in Oporto, Portugal.

W & A Gilbey remained a family business until 1962, when they merged with United Wine Traders Ltd to form International Distillers and Vintners Ltd. Ten years later the company was taken over by the brewing firm Watney Mann Ltd, and in the same year Grand Metropolitan Hotels acquired Watneys. A final merger in 1997 of GrandMet and Guinness created Diageo plc.

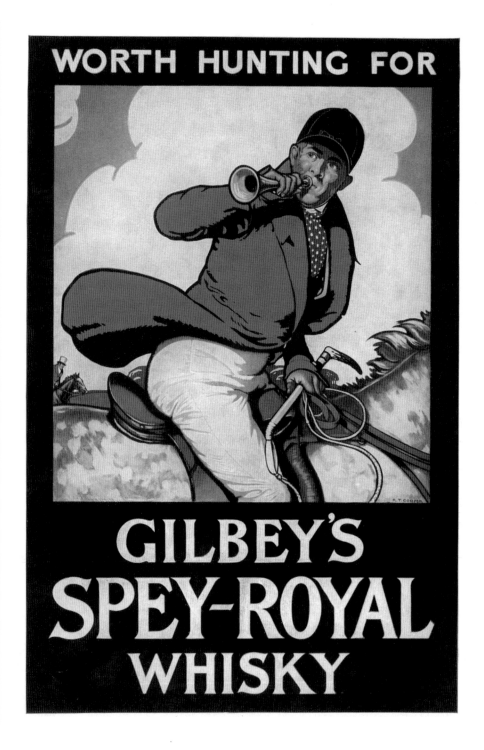

1922. *Spey Royal* was regularly advertised during the 1920s and 1930s.

(left) 1924.

1926.

1937. The blend was improved and 'Guaranteed Ten Years Old'.

1937. *Spey Royal*'s successful development and popularity was partly attributed to its special square amber bottle, unchanged from when it was introduced in 1896.

1938. From the series of 'Stories of the Clans'.

1957. A full-page advertisement in *The Illustrated London News* shows the embossed bottle which replaced the original square amber bottle of 1896.

1950. An advertisement in the *New Yorker*. In the years after the war, *Spey-Royal* became one of the company's leading export brands with considerable success in the United States. This was often in tandem with Gilbey's London Dry Gin in its unique 'frosted' bottle.

John Gillon & Co. Ltd

Thomas Rule, in partnership with Sir John Gillon of Linlithgow, established the company in Leith in 1817, trading as Gillon & Rule. Rule retired in 1826 and Gillon continued running the business as John Gillon & Co. Having suffered from the crash of Pattison's, the company merged, in 1912, with three other whisky distillers and blending firms. For a number of years the new company, Ainslie, Baillie & Co., struggled to survive, and was eventually forced into liquidation in 1921, passing into the hands of Sir James Calder and his company, Macdonald, Greenlees & Williams (Distillers) Ltd. Four years later that company was acquired by DCL.

W. Greer and Co. Ltd

William Greer was a member of an Irish distilling family and moved to Glasgow in 1893, where he established himself as a leading wine and spirit merchant. He produced blended whiskies for sale at home and overseas. The Glasgow whisky merchants, Mitchell Bros Ltd, took over the company in the early 1900s. The (Irish) Distillers Finance Corporation acquired Mitchell in 1913, and they in turn became part of DCL in 1922.

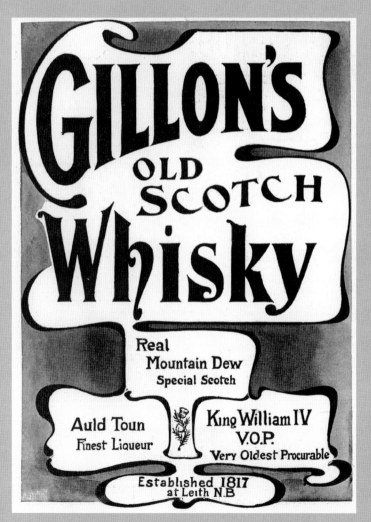

1904. An early and rare 'art nouveau' advertisement for Gillon's and its range of Old Scotch Whisky: *Real Mountain Dew Special Scotch, Auld Toun Finest Liqueur* and *King William IV V.O.P. (Very Oldest Procurable)*.

1903. A rare example of an advertisement for Greer's *10 Years Old O.V.H. Old Vatted Highland* and *15 Years Old Imperial Liqueur* whiskies.

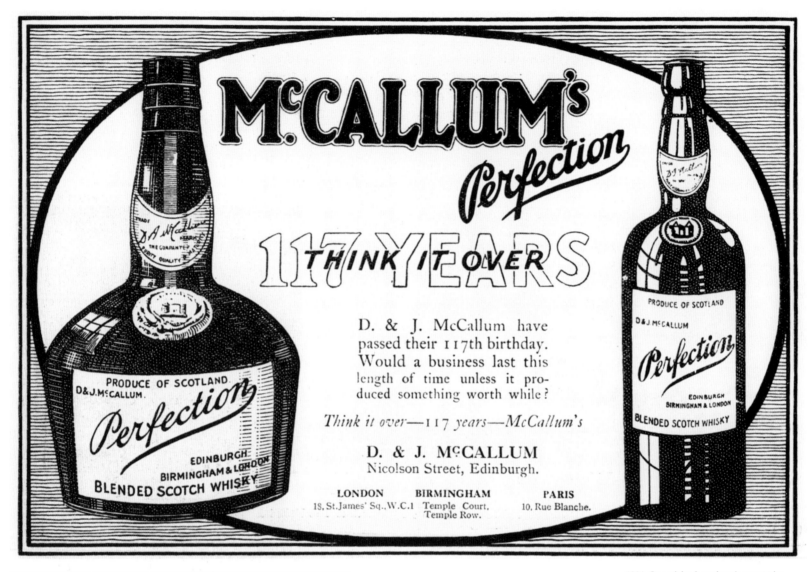

D & J McCallum Ltd

Founded in 1807 by two Edinburgh inn-keeping brothers, Duncan and John McCallum, the business eventually developed into blending whiskies, and *McCallum's Perfection Scots Whisky* sold well especially in Australia and New Zealand. The company was taken over by DCL in 1937.

1924. One of the few advertisements for *McCallum's Perfection*, and it was hardly designed to set the heather on fire! The brand has survived the rigours of time and sells well in Australia.

Macdonald Greenlees Ltd.

Macdonald Greenlees Ltd is the name given to an amalgamation of four companies acquired by DCL in 1925. The first of these companies is believed to have roots as far back as 1840, when the firm of Alexander and Macdonald was established in Leith, and they blended *Sandy Macdonald* whisky. In 1900 they built Stronachie distillery in Perthshire, and the company was bought by Sir James Calder in 1907.

In 1871, James and Samuel Greenlees set themselves up in Glasgow as whisky blenders and merchants, and developed Old Parr De Luxe whisky, successful initially in London and then enjoying good sales in Brazil and Canada in the early 1900s. In 1919 Sir James Calder acquired the company, and in the same year he took over William Williams & Sons Ltd of Aberdeen, owners of Glendullan distillery. He amalgamated the three whisky companies as Macdonald, Greenlees & Williams (Distillers) Ltd, and bought Auchinblae distillery in Kincardineshire, which had gone into liquidation in 1916. In 1925 Sir James Calder sold the company, along with his own Dalwhinnie distillery, to DCL, and it was renamed Macdonald Greenlees Ltd.

1924. Auchinblae and Stronachie distilleries were taken out of production in 1929. The original Glendullan distillery, built in 1897, survived until the 1980s when all Glendullan single malt whisky was produced in a new distillery that had been built in 1972 on an adjacent site on the river Fiddich near Dufftown.

John Robertson & Son Ltd

Established in Dundee in 1827, the company produced *J.R.D.*, a blended whisky that enjoyed considerable success. The company built Coleburn distillery, near Elgin, in 1896. John Walker & Sons Ltd, in their quest to find more stock to support their growing sales of *Johnnie Walker*, and in partnership with DCL, jointly purchased Robertson in 1915.

1893. One of the oldest whisky advertisement in the Archive. The two lines of conversation are:
Dr. N....(loquitur) 'Hilloa Scotty! You here already, and all alone?'
'Ou' ay'. I've J.R.D. wi' me, and ye' ken a' goot man and a goot whisky is goot company'.

JUNE 20, 1894. THE SKETCH. 439

JOHN ROBERTSON & SON, DUNDEE, and 4, Great Tower Street, E.C.

1894. A full-page advertisement in *The Sketch* has a strong Japanese influence.
Top row: 'He is weary. He calls. Not in vain.'
Bottom row: 'All gone. He is angry. He remembers.'
Centre: 'A certain bottle of J.R.D. whisky to his great joy.'
'Ask for John Robertson & Son's Dundee Whisky. It is the best.'

J & G Stewart Ltd (incorporating Andrew Usher & Co.)

Established in 1779 as a tea and wine merchant, James Stewart had, by the 1870s, become one of the first successful exporters of blended whisky. In 1917 DCL bought the company and its desirable 800,000 gallons of maturing whisky, valued at £2.3 million, and its established export business. It had been DCL's intention to cease selling the J & G Stewart's whisky brands in the home trade, but government regulations forced it to continue supplying them to home trade customers at half the quantity they had purchased in 1916. Thus, DCL was compelled to change its own rule of supplying blended whiskies only to overseas markets.

The firm of Andrew Usher & Co. was founded in 1819 and became the agent for Smith's Glenlivet in 1840. Usher was an early pioneer of vatting malt whiskies – *Usher's Old Vatted Glenlivet* dates back to 1853. Following the Blending Act of 1865, this brand became one of the first blended whiskies. The company bought the Glen Sciennes distillery in Edinburgh in 1859, re-naming it the Edinburgh distillery, and kept it until 1919, when it was sold to SMD. In the same year the company and its large stocks of whisky was acquired by DCL.

1909.

1910. The brand of whisky on the table is *Old Vatted Glenlivet*. It is not entirely clear what liquid the naked infant is intending to ladle into the glass!

1910. The bottom line ranks as one of the best: 'Usher's whisky is the best in "plane" or "aero"-ated water.'

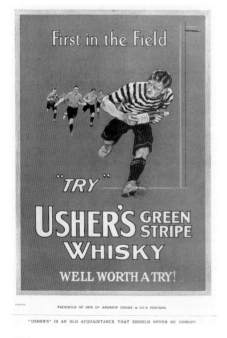

1911.

1915. A full-page advertisement illustrated by Montague Dawson in *The Graphic* of January 1915 combines a hint of patriotism with the reassuring quality of Usher's whiskies, 'Safe in all waters'. HMS *Lion*, built at Devonport in 1911, was to see action in the Battle of Dogger Bank on 24 January 1915 (six days before the appearance of this advertisement) and in the Battle of Jutland in May 1916. Although damaged in both battles, HMS *Lion* survived, and with little further combative action before the end of the war, she was eventually broken up at Jarrow under the terms of the Washington Treaty of 1922.

1922. These were the days when whisky advertising was targeted exclusively at men.

1923. Christopher Clark illustrated the 'Accomplished Equestrians' series.

James Watson and Co. Ltd

Founded in 1815 in Dundee, the company became one of the largest whisky blending houses in Scotland. It bought three distilleries – Ord in 1887, Parkmore in 1900 and Pulteney in 1920 – and developed *Watson's No.10* as a very successful high-quality blend, which became a leading brand in Australia. In 1923, J.J. Watson, the elderly owner of this private company, wished to retire from the business, and instructed his managing director, Thomas Herd, later to become the chairman of DCL to find a buyer. The company, with its three distilleries and 5.5 million gallons of whisky, was at first offered to DCL, who, not requiring this amount of stock, asked the 'Big Three', Buchanan-Dewar and Walkers, if they wished to participate. Their response was positive. They wanted the stock and the distilleries, but because *Watson's No.10* competed with their own brands, they would take it off the market. The DCL disapproved of that intention and withdrew from the negotiations. The 'Big Three' went ahead and bought the company, and two years later the group of companies amalgamated with DCL.

1906.

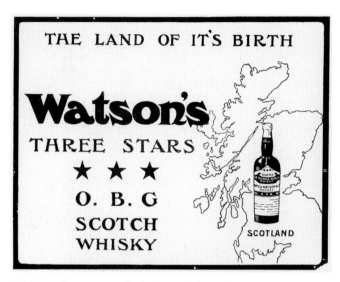

1906. It's an all too common mistake that can lurk round any corner.

1907. *Watson's Three Starts Whisky* is a blend of old Glenlivet whiskies.

   George Smith built *The* Glenlivet distillery in Glen Livet in 1824. He died in 1871 and was succeeded by his son, John Gordon Smith. By then Glenlivet was firmly established as the most successful whisky in London. J.G. Smith was concerned that many distilleries were incorporating 'Glenlivet' in the name of their distilleries and their whiskies. After a great deal of legal action it was eventually ruled in 1884 that Smith's Glenlivet distillery was the only one entitled to be called *The* Glenlivet, and that a further ten distilleries were allowed to use Glenlivet but only as a suffix to the distillery name. Macallan, Glenfarclas, Linkwood and Aberlour are four examples of Glenlivets that would have probably have been used in *Watson's Old Blended Glenlivet Whisky.*

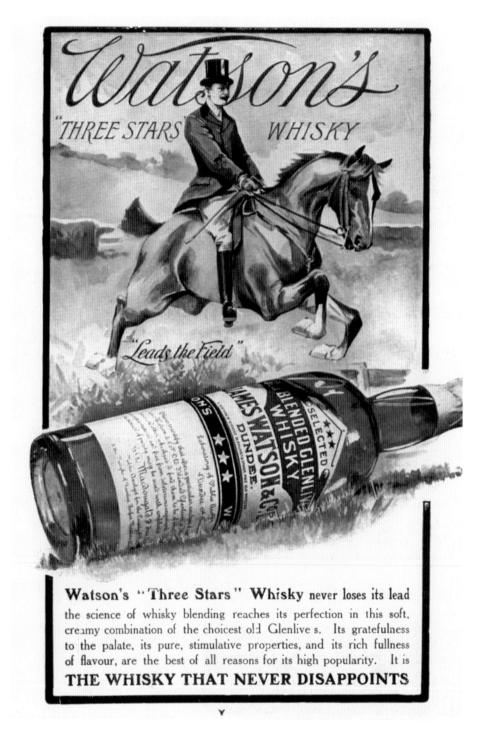

Watson's "Three Stars" Whisky never loses its lead the science of whisky blending reaches its perfection in this soft, creamy combination of the choicest old Glenlivets. Its gratefulness to the palate, its pure, stimulative properties, and its rich fullness of flavour, are the best of all reasons for its high popularity. It is **THE WHISKY THAT NEVER DISAPPOINTS**

Around 1905. *Watson's Blue Band.*

1910. An advertisement that exudes extraordinary smugness!

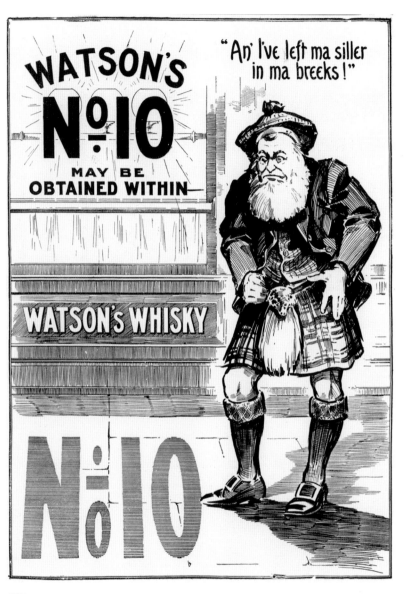

1905.

1905. Watson's most successful brand: *Watson's No. 10.*

1907

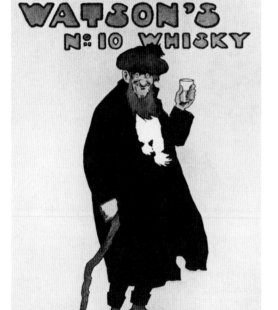

1909. A Will Owen cartoon.

1909. The Royal Commission that examined 'Whisky and other Potable Spirits' leading to its report in 1909 defining 'What is whisky?', regularly used an 'e' in whisky – 'whiskey' – a spelling that was common then but is now restricted to Irish and American whiskey. Watson's turned the boy's simple topical question into a delightful cartoon drawn by John Hassall.

TWO GREAT PREMIERS

THE PREMIER
1868 & 1874-1880

Earl of Beaconsfield, Benjamin Disraeli (1804-1881) became Premier in 1868 and again in 1874. One of England's most popular statesmen and a succesful novelist. He passed a bill conferring the title of Empress of India on Queen Victoria, and firmly established British influence in the East.

"Premier"

The Whisky de Luxe

**THE 'PREMIER'
OF TO-DAY.**

is a spirit of great delicacy, having a creamy smoothness and charming bouquet which irresistibly appeals to the sensitive and fastidious palate. Of full strength yet beautifully light, it is, indeed, the Premier of Scotch Whiskies.

WRIGHT & GREIG, LTD.,
DISTILLERS OF
"RODERICK DHU."
GLASGOW & LONDON.

Wright and Greig Ltd

Established in Glasgow in the 1890s, Wright & Greig became a leading Glasgow firm of whisky blenders, and developed a very successful export market for their *Roderick Dhu* and *Premier* blended whiskies, especially in India, Australia and New Zealand. In 1900 the company bought Dallas Dhu distillery on Speyside from Alexander Edward, who had built the distillery the previous year. The company suffered badly from the collapse of Pattison, and was forced into liquidation in 1919. Dallas Dhu was sold to Benmore Distilleries Ltd, which was duly acquired by DCL in 1929.

1916. The last advertisement from the Archive is of a brand lost in the mists of time: *Wright & Greig's Premier Extra Old Scotch Whisky – The Whisky de Luxe*, and for good measure the bottom label states: 'This Whisky is the very finest that can be produced'. Furthermore, it 'is a spirit of great delicacy, having a creamy smoothness and charming bouquet which irresistibly appeals to the sensitive and fastidious palate. Of full strength yet beautifully light, it is, indeed, the Premier of Scotch Whiskies'. Who could fail to enjoy it? And all at a time when Europe was engaged in the worst of all wars.

Chapter 10
The Artists

JAMES BUCHANAN & CO., LTD., 26, HOLBORN, LONDON, E.C.1.

Cecil Charles Windsor Aldin

Born in 1870 in Slough, Berkshire, Aldin's art training led him to specialise – using most media except oils – as a sporting artist and an illustrator of posters and advertisements for many of the leading companies, such as Colman's, Bovril and Player's cigarettes. In 1898 he was co-founder, with Phil May, Tom Browne, Lance Thackeray and Dudley Hardy, of the London Sketch Club. Aldin developed a passion for hunting and in 1914 became Master of the South Berkshire Foxhounds. In addition to writing a number of books and illustrating many others, Aldin designed toys, greetings cards, postcards, wallpaper for Liberty and Sanderson's, and produced designs used by Royal Doulton.

Aldin died in 1935 and his obituary in *The Times* stated that he: 'was one of the leading spirits in the renaissance of the British sporting artist'.

Tom Browne

Tom Browne was born in Nottingham on 8 December 1870, and left school aged eleven to work as an errand boy. At fourteen he became apprenticed to a lithographic printer. His first drawing was published in *Scraps* when he was nineteen. In 1895 he moved to London and created the two tramps, Weary Willy and Tired Tim, who first appeared in *Illustrated Chips* in 1896, continuing for the next fifty-seven years until the publication folded in 1953. Browne established his own colour-printing company in 1897, and designed many advertisements and postcards. He was a painter in oils and watercolours, and many of his subjects were of Dutch

scenes. He was one of the five founder members of the London Sketch Club and was its president in 1907. Browne contributed to *Punch* and a number of other magazines and journals, and spent some time in the United States. On 16 March 1910 he died of throat cancer at the age of thirty-nine, less than two years after he had created the *Johnnie Walker* striding man that was to become one of the most recognised advertising subjects of the twentieth century.

Leopold Alfred Cheney

Leo Cheney was a bank clerk in Accrington, Lancashire, and in 1905 became the first pupil of Percy Bradshaw's Press Art School correspondence course. He sold his first sporting illustrations to the *Manchester Evening News* in 1907, and shortly afterwards became staff sports cartoonist and caricaturist on the paper. For two years in the early 1920s he worked as political cartoonist for the *Daily Mail* in London. Cheney's work for *Johnnie Walker* began at the outbreak of the First World War, producing a series of patriotic war cartoons, the first advertisement to show clearly *Johnnie Walker Black Label*, a post-war 'Travel' series and four further series of advertisements. His last series was completed in 1927, and he died in September the following year.

Christopher Clark

Christopher Clark was born in 1875 and lived in London. He specialised in illustrating and painting military and historical subjects. During the 1920s he produced many advertisements for *John Haig*, and in the early 1930s, for *Black & White*. He produced many poster designs, often with a military or pageantry theme, many of which were for railway companies. He died in 1942.

Alfred Chantrey Corbould

Born in London's Kensington in 1852, A.C. Corbould was the son of the portrait painter Alfred Hitchens Corbould, and grandson of Henry Corbould, designer of Queen Victoria's portrait for the first-ever postage stamps in 1840.

From 1871 he was a regular contributor of hunting and countryside cartoons to *Punch*. He joined the *Daily Graphic* in 1890 and contributed sporting cartoons to a wide range of magazines. He died in 1920.

Morgan Dennis

Morgan Dennis was born in Boston, Massachusetts, in 1892. He was educated at the New School of Design in Boston, and studied etching in Provincetown. He worked for ten years with newspapers in Boston, until drawing dogs became his main interest. He died in 1960.

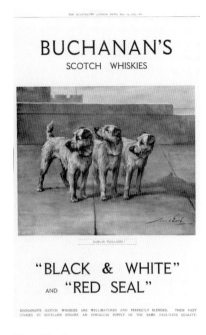

Maud Earl

Maud Earl was born in London in 1864, the only child of George Earl, a talented painter of sporting pastimes. Earl was taught by her father, and at the Royal Female School of Art. She specialised in dog paintings and exhibited her first work at the Royal Academy in 1884. Her work received high acclaim and she painted dogs belonging to Queen Victoria and King Edward VII. In 1920 she established a studio in Paris, and a few years later emigrated to the United States where her success continued. Around the turn of the century many of her paintings were engraved and her studies of many breeds of dogs provide a valuable and historical record. Earl died in New York in 1943, and is considered as perhaps the pre-eminent painter of purebred dogs.

Fougasse (Cyril Kenneth Bird)

Born on 17 December 1887 in London, the son of an iron merchant and cricketer, Arthur Bird. Bird trained as an engineer at King's College, London, and took evening art classes. He was a machine-gun instructor and, after a period employed at the Rosyth naval base, he served in the Royal Engineers during the First World War. He was invalided out and began drawing cartoons as 'Fougasse', the name of an anti-personnel mine: '... its effectiveness is not always reliable and its aim uncertain!'

Bird contributed cartoons often depicting motoring and radio subjects to various magazines. In 1937 he was appointed Art Editor of *Punch*, and between 1949 and 1953 he was the only cartoonist to hold the post as Editor. An air-raid warden during the Second World War, he designed posters and cartoons for government departments, and perhaps his most memorable series was the wartime Ministry of Information 'Careless Talk' posters. His work had a distinctive, strikingly economical style using few lines, and is immediately recognisable. He died in June 1965.

John Hassall

John Hassall was born in Kent in 1868 and, failing to be accepted by the Royal Military Academy at Sandhurst, he moved to Canada and farmed with his brother. When, in 1890, his first published drawing appeared in the *Daily Graphic*, he returned to the UK and took advice from his friend, Dudley Hardy, and studied art, firstly in Antwerp and then in Paris. After four years he returned to London and started his own art school, the New Art School and School of Poster Design, later known as the John Hassall School of Art, which he ran for twenty years. Hassall was one of the founder members of the London Sketch Club and was a prolific producer of theatrical posters and posters for railway companies, the London Underground and many other clients. He illustrated numerous books, produced wallpaper designs, drew some of the earliest postcard designs and designed pottery for Royal Doulton. He will always be remembered for his classic 1908 advertisement, 'Skegness is So Bracing', featuring the jolly fisherman skipping along the beach. He died in 1948.

Rowland Hilder

Rowland Hilder was born in Long Island, USA, in 1905, and moved to England when he was ten years old. He studied for five years at Goldsmiths College School of Art and was a landscape and marine painter, illustrator and poster artist. He wrote books on watercolour techniques and is well known for illustrations of the British countryside, especially scenes centred on Kentish oast houses. He died in 1993.

Leonard Raven Hill

Born in Bath in 1867, Leonard Raven Hill studied at the Lambeth School of Art and, while still a student, he had his first joke cartoons published in *Judy*. From 1885 to 1887 he studied art in Paris, exhibiting at the Paris Salon at the age of twenty. On his return to Britain he worked as a painter but had more success contributing joke cartoons and illustrations to a wide range of magazines. He worked for several publications until joining *Punch* in 1901. He succeeded Bernard Partridge as Second Cartoonist in 1910, and drew political cartoons until he retired in 1935. He designed advertisements for a number of companies and drew two series of advertisements for *Johnnie Walker* between 1912 and 1913. He died in 1942.

Sir Osbert Lancaster

Born in London in 1908, Osbert Lancaster studied at the Byam Shaw School of Art before studying English at Lincoln College, Oxford. With only a fourth-class degree he returned to studying art at Oxford's Ruskin School, and then studied stage design at the Slade.

In his very full and varied life, Lancaster designed posters, wrote and illustrated many books, and was a political cartoonist, illustrator, theatre designer and painter. He is famous for his single column 'pocket' cartoons that appeared on the front page of the *Daily Express* featuring Maudie, Countess of Littlehampton, and it is estimated that over the period 1939 to 1981, he drew in excess of 10,000 cartoons. Knighted in 1975, Sir Osbert Lancaster died in Chelsea in 1986.

Frank Henry Mason

Born in County Durham in 1875, Frank Mason was a marine engineer, and then trained as an artist at the Scarborough School of Art. He became a marine artist in oils and watercolours, and was a prolific producer of artwork for the posters used by the regional railway companies. He died in 1965.

Will Owen

Born in Malta in 1869, William Owen was the son of a British Naval Officer. The family settled back in Kent and after school Owen studied at the Lambeth School of Art, and at Heatherley's. While working at the London headquarters of the Post Office Savings Bank, he contributed cartoons and illustrations to a number of magazines. He spent two years in France before the First World War broke out. On his return he established himself as a commercial artist, and produced many poster and postcard designs. His most famous creations were the Bisto kids in the gravy advertisement 'Ah, Bisto!' and 'Bovril puts BEEF into you'. He had several books published and was a broadcaster on radio, hosting the BBC's *Children's Hour*. He died in 1957.

117

Sir Bernard Partridge

Born in London in 1861, Bernard Partridge , the youngest son of Professor Richard Partridge, Professor of the Royal College of Surgeons, left school to work at an architect's office, and then spent two years with a firm of ecclesiastical designers. He studied decorative painting and then attended two art schools, before working as a decorator of church interiors and then as a professional actor appearing in the first production of Bernard Shaw's 'Arms and the Man'. His first cartoons were published in 1885 and he joined the staff of *Punch* in 1891. Partridge subsequently worked for the magazine for fifty years. He was their Second Cartoonist from 1899, and then Cartoonist from 1910 until his death in 1945. He produced political and joke cartoons as well as theatrical caricatures for the magazine, and freelance designs of advertisements for a number of leading companies. His first work for *Johnnie Walker* was published in December 1910 in the style of Tom Browne.

Charles Pears

Charles Pears was born in Pontefract, Yorkshire, in 1873. He was educated at a local college and contributed theatrical sketches to *The Yorkshireman* in 1895. Two years later Pears moved to London and began his career as an illustrator and caricaturist in the theatrical world. He contributed drawings to many magazines and designed posters and advertisements for many companies, including *Black & White* whisky. Pears developed an interest in painting maritime subjects and founded the Society of Naval Artists. He served in the Royal Marines in the First World War, and was the official war artist to the Admiralty from 1915 to 1918, and for most of the Second World War. He had several books published and illustrated a large number of books, including the works of Dickens. He moved to Cornwall in his later years and died in Truro in 1958.

Frank Reynolds

Frank Reynolds was born in London in 1876. He studied at Heatherley's and contributed comic drawings to a number of magazines. In the early years of the twentieth century, he became a staff artist on *The Illustrated London News* and *The Sketch*, and developed an interest in painting watercolours. In 1919 he joined the staff of *Punch* and was its Art Editor for ten years. Reynolds was president of the London Sketch Club in 1909, and again in 1922, and established his reputation as an illustrator of books with his 1910 Gift Book edition of *Pickwick Papers*.

Clive Uptton

Clive Upton was born in London in 1911. He studied at both the Southend and Central Schools of Art and had a long and successful career as a political cartoonist, illustrator, caricaturist, poster artist and landscape and portrait painter. In the 1930s he added an extra 't' to his name, to differentiate himself from another illustrator with the same surname.

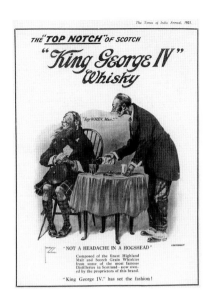

Arthur Wardle

Arthur Wardle was born in London in 1864. Largely self-taught, he became well known as an animal artist, with his first work exhibited at the Royal Academy when he was sixteen. He painted all types of animals but is probably best known for his dog subjects. He used watercolours, pastels and oils, and some of his best work combined the use of chalks and watercolours. He died in 1949.

Lawson Wood

Clarence Lawson Wood was born in Highgate, London, in 1878, the son of landscape painter Pinhorn Wood. He studied art at the Slade, Heatherley's, and at Frank Calderon's School of Animal Painting. He joined Pearson's, a magazine publisher, and became its chief artist. He left after six years to freelance, designing posters, drawing cartoons and postcards, and designing and making wooden toys.

Lawson Wood is perhaps best remembered for his humorous animal subjects, especially Gran'pop, the artful ginger ape. He illustrated books and had many of his own books published, including, from 1935, the Gran'pop Annuals. He died in 1957.

Doris Clare Zinkeisen

Doris Zinkeisen was born in Kilcreggan, Dumbartonshire, Scotland, in 1898, and studied at the Harrow School of Art and the Royal Academy. She was primarily a designer of theatrical sets and costumes. She specialised in society portraits and designed a few posters for the LNER. In 1927 Zinkeisen designed *Johnnie Walker*'s first series of colour advertisements for use in magazines, with subjects and execution that were to mark a radical move away from the previous conventional style. She died in 1991.

Selected Bibliography

Andrews, Allen, *The Whisky Barons* (Jupiter, 1977)

Barnard, Alfred, *Whisky Distilleries of the United Kingdom* (Harper's Weekly Gazette, 1887)

Bryant, Mark, *Dictionary of Twentieth-Century British Cartoonists and Caricaturists* (Ashgate, 2000)

Daiches, David, *Scotch Whisky, Its Past and Present* (André Deutsch, 1969)

D.C.L. Gazette – various

Hume, John R. & Moss, Michael S., *The Making of Scotch Whisky* (Canongate, 2000)

Kidd, Jane, *Gilbeys, Wine and Horses* (The Lutterworth Press, 1997)

Laver, James, *The House of Haig* (John Haig & Co. Ltd, 1958)

McDowall, R.J.S., *The Whiskies of Scotland* (John Murray, 1967)

Murray, Jim, *The Art of Whisky* (Public Record Office Publications, 1998)

Morrice, Philip, *The Schweppes Guide to Scotch* (Alphabooks, 1983)

Nevett, T.R., *Advertising in Britain* (Heinemann, on behalf of the History of Advertising Trust, 1982)

Smith, Gavin D., *A Book of Words: Whisky* (Carcanet 1993)

Weir, R.B., *The History of the Distillers Company 1877-1939* (Clarendon Press, 1995)

Wilson, Neil, *Scotch and Water* (Lochar, 1985)

Wilson, Ross, *The House of Sanderson* (Wm. Sanderson, 1963)